Jonathan Okinaga is a friend and inspiration. His story of alcohol and drug abuse has become a message of hope from despair. He knows the pit, and he found how to get out of it. Addiction can be beat, and this book will show you how.

Jim Burns, Ph.D.
President, HomeWord
Author of *Confident Parenting, Creating an Intimate Marriage*

I love it honestly. The sincerity and raw emotion is so real. The love in your heart for all of us hurting is refreshing.

Grace H

Each person has a story to be told. Jon speaks from a place where the struggle of obedience is ultimately won out by his love for God and the desire to serve Him. This is a daily struggle, and Jon's transparency serves to remind us all about the challenge that ministry presents. God bless you, Jon. Keep fighting the good fight.

Jon Motohiro
Marriage and Family Therapist

This book is a must read for anyone fighting the battle for sobriety or those with a loved one waging that war. It gives true insight into the nature of the disease along with the steps needed to achieve the cure. As a recovering alcoholic, this will hold a permanent, prominent place in my library.

Frank B

Jon's sharing of many intimate details of his life is proof of his sincerity to help others in similar circumstances. He has emerged victorious in his battle. This text is a powerful encouragement for others to do the same.

Leonard Lawyer

How God Sanitized My Soul

Written by
Jonathan Okinaga

Publishing

Published by
Innovo Publishing, LLC
www.innovopublishing.com
1-888-546-2111

Providing Full-Service Publishing Services for
Christian Organizations & Authors: Hardbacks, Paperbacks,
eBooks, Audio Books, & iPhone Application Books

How God Sanitized My Soul

Biblical quotes are from the New International Version of the Bible.
Copyright © 1973, 1978, 1984 by Biblica.

ISBN 13: 978-1-936076-14-7
ISBN 10: 1-936076-14-4

Cover Design & Interior Layout: Innovo Publishing, LLC

Printed in the United States of America
U.S. Printing History

First Edition: December 2009

Dedication

One of the reasons I started sanitizeyoursoul.org, which eventually led to this book, is Tait, a good friend with whom I had gone through rehab. Tait was my roommate. We'd had the same case manager, were on the same track, and had spent countless hours just talking about life. He left residential treatment a week before I did, but I continued to see him at various meetings that we attended. Every time I saw him, he'd hug me and say, "I love you, man." The last time I saw him, he was driving away from the transitional house (the next step after residential treatment), and he had the saddest, most downtrodden look I've ever seen. In retrospect, I think he knew that was to be our final goodbye. Three days later, Tait slit his wrist and died, only a few blocks from the center.

Processing Tait's suicide was hard. The day before he died, I had missed a phone call from him. Still in the early stages of my own sobriety, I was a flake and didn't see the importance of calling him back. I beat myself up over his passing, but I now know that I was in no position to have made a difference.

That first night, while coping with newly found emotions— genuine feelings that weren't drug-induced—my sponsor asked me what I was going to do. My reply: "I'll do whatever I can to one day be in a position to help those struggling with addiction. If I can play a role in keeping even one family from going through what Tait's family is going through, I'll do it."

It's been over two years since that sad day, and what I've never shared until now is a letter I wrote to Tait....

Dear Tait,

Dude, I wish I had picked up that phone call. Unfortunately, I was in no position to help you that night. I was still a selfish, self-centered drunk who wanted to watch a movie instead of walk outside to talk to you. I am so sorry.

You were the first real friend I met in rehab (even though my first impression was that you didn't like me). For all those cigarettes we shared on the balcony late at night...thanks. It made me realize that I wasn't alone—that someone actually understood me.

It's kind of a catch-22 for me. If we hadn't been so close and you were still alive, would I be sober? Would I have seen that addictions really kill? What would I be doing with my life? I finally stopped asking those questions, and I just want to let you know... I miss you. With Christ as my source of strength and wisdom, I hope to never lose another friend the way I lost you.

I can only hope that when you look down from heaven and see me working my tail off, you'll know that I still think of you. Whenever I feel like quitting my ministry, whenever there are doubts about why I do my job, or any hesitancy on my part to call and help addicts... your name, face, smile, and laugh will come to mind. Tait—a life that ended way too soon, but one that made a lasting impression on me. Miss ya, homie.

Jon

Acknowledgments

A common phrase in the book is, "On my own I am an idiot, but with God as my source of strength, amazing things happen." All the glory goes to Christ. Without His sacrificial death on the cross, I would never understand faith, hope, and love. I am blessed with a family that shows love beyond words. Dad, Mom, Marissa, Shelby, grandparents, aunts, uncles, and cousins, I love you. Without your prayers, I would be dead. You are daily reminders of what a Christian family is supposed to look like. Even though I strayed so far, you never gave up on me. Thank you. To those who have helped me from my very earliest steps to sobriety: Ty Estrada, Stew Lewis, Mike Redinger, Ed Hardy, Stephen Heard, and Nina Dryer, you helped this broken man, destined for certain death, to slowly rebuild his life. I have mentors who have invested countless hours helping to mold me into the man I am today. Wisdom can be found in the Bible, and these men showed me how to apply it in practical ways: Tim Pappas, Vaughn Brown, Dr. Jim Burns, Pastor Robert Miller, Pastor David Giomi, Pastor Kaala Souza, Pastor Buzzy Enniss, and Pastor Eric Bothello. You have all set the standard as men of God.

Thank you, my Hawaii friends, who lift me up when I am weak. There are so many, but a special thanks goes to Jaclyn Park, Matt Chun, Briana Sugihara, Tiffani Tanaka, Marci Masuda, Jon Motohiro, Chris Smith, Natalie Choy, Leonard Lawyer, Cori Saito, and Kelsie Okamura. When I came back from rehab, you guys were the ones who planned sober activities and supported me unconditionally. You are all blessings from God. To the California crew that inspired me to step out in faith and start a community in Hawaii: you are my second family. I'm keeping up the anonymity part so it's first name, last initial: Andrew M, Frank B, John M,

Karen S, Jamie G, Grace H, Matt P, Megan M, Joel R, and countless others. Even though we are 2,500 miles apart, you never seem that far away.

Last but not least are the churches and prayer warriors that help make my sobriety and ministry possible: Waialae Baptist Church, Hope Chapel Manaolana, Sanctuary Faith Community, and theeffect. Thank you.

Foreword

For over 365 days I bared my soul for anyone to read. What is written in these pages is my life story: family & friends, childhood to who I am today, my struggles with addiction, and how I overcame it.

Each day is a blessing; with every person I meet there has been a learning experience. Is there anything I would do differently since I started sanitizeyoursoul.org? No. Through the good and bad, happiness and pain, times where I have failed to be an example of success…everything that happened was in God's will.

As I try to summarize the last year of my life, all I can say is that I'm grateful for everything. My life was always full of doubt, frustration, disappointment, and fear. I still have moments when those feelings return; now I know how to get past them and find love, joy, peace, patience, kindness, goodness, faithfulness, humility, and self control.

I'm able to get over my demons by relying on Christ. I pray, read the Bible, and help others DAILY. If there is one scripture that has spoken to me the most it would be, "For God so loved the world that He gave His one and only Son, that whoever believes in Him shall not perish but have eternal life." John 3:16

There has to be a reason that this is the most recognized verse in the Bible. A clear reminder that despite all my shortcomings, regardless of how I fall short of the glory of God, in spite of my failures, even though at one time I was a raging alcoholic with drug addiction…God still loved me so much that He sent His only Son to die so that I may live.

This second chance in life is only possible because of Jesus. I will never be like Christ but I can strive to be Christ-like: loving the unlovable, giving hope to the hopeless, sharing peace to those in a chaotic world, being patient with those who don't deserve it, showing kindness and goodness to people who are used to despair and pain.

At one point I felt unlovable, hopeless, chaotic, and undeserving of anything good; the pain and despair nearly killed me. No drug, drink, meeting, woman, money, fame, or power could ever have fixed me. It has been my personal relationship with Christ that has healed those wounds. As you read what God has placed on my heart, please know that without Him I am nothing, but because of Him I can share with you *...How God Sanitized My Soul.*

Table of Contents

INTRODUCTION

I've always had a problem dealing with emotions and feelings. Drinking and using drugs were how I hid from things I couldn't or didn't want to express or feel. Over a few years I watched my once vibrant mother suffer from a rare neurological disease. Both of my grandfathers passed away within a span of only three months. To say that I was angry at God is an understatement.

In time I became involved in the nightclub scene. Because I knew the bar owners and head bartenders, I was treated like a king. Satan was in control and I didn't care. My involvement grew deeper as I began working as a club promoter. I was living the life of a rock star and was enjoying every moment. Little did I know it would eventually consume my life and turn me into a monster. Soon after I arrived on the scene, drinking wasn't enough so I progressed to marijuana, pills, ecstasy, and cocaine. I had become the poster boy for Satan's destructive power. Unfulfilled relationships, untapped potential, utter hopelessness and, most damaging of all, a non-existent walk with Christ.

Despite being raised in the church, attending numerous conventions, even being a Sunday school teacher at one point, I was living a life far from the cross. All the Bible knowledge was there; it was just lost in the fog of drugs and alcohol. How can one fall so far from the mercy and grace of God? By falling for the many traps that Satan puts before us. There is a quote that explains what I now know to be true that says, "Fame is fleeting. Money comes and goes. Popularity is an accident. The only thing that remains is character."

I had hit rock bottom and desperately needed help. *Desperately*. It came in the form of my admittance into a rehab facility in California. After I checked in and went through the routine paperwork and introductory process, the worker said he didn't know how I was still alive. That night I got on my knees and prayed a simple prayer. I asked God to take away all yearnings for drugs and alcohol; otherwise, I didn't want to wake up. If I woke up the next morning, then one day I would share how my miracle of sobriety was a gift from God.

Not surprisingly, rehab wasn't all that fun, but I'm not ashamed to say that I spent two months with alcoholics and addicts. Out of all the people I went through rehab with, I'm the only one since leaving rehab in July 2007, who hasn't relapsed. A few of them ended up in jail, a couple of them were sent to mental institutions, and two of them committed suicide. As an addict, I've learned that I need to live a disciplined life. Discipline is defined as "training that corrects, molds, or perfects mental faculties or moral character."

The joy of the Lord is my strength. I live my life in sobriety with a joy and peace that were never around when I was drinking and using drugs. The same hurts and frustrations are still there; the only difference is that now I turn to God to help me get through the day. When making decisions I keep things simple: love, joy, peace, patience, kindness, goodness, faithfulness, humility, and self-control. The Fruit of the Spirit needs to be the foundation of my life because without it, I'm not walking in accordance with the Word of God and my soul suffers the consequences.

Because I'm human I still fall short of the glory of God, but instead of feeling condemnation and guilt, I ask for forgiveness and experience the freedom that comes from the grace of Christ. I used to question why I'm the only one who has been successful on the other side of rehab. The answer is simple: God. I had countless people praying for me, and I rejected the lie that I did this on my own. Without the continued prayer and support of my family, church family, and friends, I would not be where I am today. While others have gone the 12-Step route or their own path, I've decided to follow Jesus. There is the old hymn, "I have decided to follow Jesus, no turning back. Though none go with me, I still will follow." That is how I live my life in sobriety.

My heart breaks when I see TV shows like *Intervention* and *Celebrity Rehab*. They advocate that you need to come to a god of your own understanding, a higher power. Some choose a doorknob or the third moon goddess from Jupiter, but until you actively seek God and ask Jesus to become your Lord and Savior, no amount of money or treatment will give you the power to overcome a sickness that ultimately leads to death. The moment one seeks God, victory is within reach because "I can do all things through Christ who strengthens me." Philippians 4:13

I believe God has called me to fight for all my brothers and sisters to help them win the battle against an enemy who is doing everything in his power to destroy us. I pray that my efforts aren't in vain and that they don't lose this difficult battle. I hope to help others who are willing to arrive at a place where they admit that they are powerless and need help—not from just "a higher power", but from Jesus Christ, my Lord and Savior.

Faithfulness   July 1st, 2008

"Faith is progressive. Faith never gets into a bad situation and says, 'I'm just going to sit here and die. It's over.' Faith never stands in the desert having a pity party with everything drying up around it. You walk by faith. You don't stand still drowning in your misery. When you get in a wilderness, you keep walking. You keep going forward even if you're only making an inch of progress with each step. When you get into battles, you have to keep saying, 'I will move forward.'" (*Fasting* by Jentezen Franklin)

Regardless of my gifts, and even if most things have come easily, I had reached a point of feeling hopeless and fear took over. That's what Satan wanted me to feel. However, God promises that I can do anything with His help.

I ran from God's mercy and grace. I was even mad at Him for situations I had put myself in. But that was okay because, unlike humans, He loves and forgives us regardless of how much we disobey him. It's called agape love. I stopped thinking about how horrible my life seemed and gave God another chance. He loves me more than I can put into words.

"But without faith it is impossible to please Him, for he who comes to God must believe that He is, and that He is the rewarder of those who diligently seek Him." Hebrews 11:6

It's easy to give up on God and return to our sinful nature. The ways of the world are so appealing; we can gain immediate satisfaction. That's the trick of Satan—it's immediate but short-lived; the rewards from God are eternal. They may not bring immediate fruit (although sometimes He blesses us more quickly than we expect), but when the fruit begins to blossom, it lasts forever.

God doesn't ask for perfection; in fact, all He asks is that we seek Him. Today you may feel that because of failure God doesn't want anything to do with you. That is so far from the truth. Seek first the kingdom of God and His righteousness and all things will be given to you. We all fall short of the glory of God. When making decisions today, realize that He doesn't want perfection; He wants us to seek Him.

Goodness   *July 1st, 2008*

"Whoever can be trusted with very little can also be trusted with much, and whoever can be dishonest with very little will be dishonest with much." Luke 16:10

The one thing that sobriety has taught me is the value of honesty. There were countless times when I was asked about drug and alcohol abuse. Each time I lied through my teeth. "Nope, not me, I would never touch the stuff." All it got me was deeper and deeper into the hole. Even to those I cared and loved about I couldn't be honest because I wasn't honest with myself.

I just finished a fast and was shown so many things. While fasting, I was asking God for guidance on a lot of issues. A main request was for Him to surround me with people I can trust with the big things that are coming up in my life. I may not like the answers He's given, but I need to be honest with myself that the more I try to fight against God's answers, the more frustrated I become. If I can't be trusted with obeying him from the beginning, how can He trust blessing me in bigger things?

Humility   July 1st, 2008

"Do nothing out of rivalry or conceit, but in humility consider others as more important than yourselves." Philippians 2:3

Humility is the lack of self-pride. Ever heard the saying, "Pride goeth before a fall?" Having a servant's heart is essential because that is exactly what Christ did. When the disciples were gathered before Jesus was arrested, what did Jesus do? He washed their feet—even the feet of Judas who was to betray him! Here was the Son of God, down on His hands and knees doing what, at the time, was considered one of the lowliest and most demeaning things to do. Remember, back then no one had shoes; the feet of the disciples must have been disgusting. However, Christ talked the talk and walked the walk. Humble yourself before God; be humble in all that you do. Remember that meekness doesn't equal weakness; the meek shall inherit the earth.

Peace   July 1st, 2008

"And the peace of God, which surpasses every thought, will guard your hearts and your minds in Christ Jesus." Philippians 4:7

Everything that happens in life has a purpose. Every prayer is heard. Every thought that we think, He knows. Sometimes it feels like He just isn't listening—that He has forgotten about us. Those are the lies that Satan wants us to believe. God, in His infinite wisdom, is in control. It's when we rebel and go against the Word of God that we fall deeper into despair.

Realize that until we are fully broken and fall before our Creator, He cannot and will not bless us. He loves us so much that His Son died on the cross for our sins. His love is unconditional, unrelenting, and omnipotent. Really search your heart and soul; you will be amazed at the peace God has in store for you.

Patience   *July 1st, 2008*

"They that wait upon the Lord shall renew their strength. They shall mount up with wings like eagles. They shall run and not be weary; they shall walk and not faint." Isaiah 40:31

This past week I've been drained—I mean going to bed around 9:30, waking up throughout the night. So why did I pick this verse? Usually when your defenses are down is the time Satan chooses to attack; this time was no different. I was having issues with work, personal life, family, you name it. This week was brutal. My normal reaction would have been to drink and do as many drugs as possible to escape my emotions. I even had a dream about relapsing. The biggest change in me was relying on God for strength to get me through tough times.

How can you apply this verse to your life? Like I stated before, many of our failures come when we are at our weakest point. It's in these times that God wants us to come to Him. What we must understand and realize is that it's in these times that we NEED Him. The next time things get rough, trust the Lord with all your heart. Have faith that He will answer your prayer for help.

How I Got and Stayed Sober   July 2nd, 2008

"Let the weak say, 'I'm strong.'" (Joel 3:10) Let the oppressed say, 'I'm free.' Let the sick say, 'I'm healed.' Let the poor say, 'I'm well off.'

How did I get sober?

"He will transform the body of our humble condition into the likeness of His glorious body by the power that enables Him to subject everything to Himself." Philippians 3:21

I had hit rock bottom and needed help, eventually ending up at a treatment facility in California. After I went through the signing-in process, the worker told me he didn't know how I was still alive. That night I got on my hands and knees and prayed a simple prayer. I asked God to take away all yearnings for drugs and alcohol; otherwise, I didn't want to wake up. And if I did wake up the next morning, I would one day share how my miracle of sobriety was a gift from God.

How do I stay sober?

"Whoever loves instruction loves knowledge, but one who hates correction is stupid." Proverbs 12:1

I changed the mentality of fighting this disease. Instead of saying, "Hi, I'm Jon, and I'm an alcoholic," I say, "I'm a recovered alcoholic by the grace of God." I don't need to be giving Satan a hold in my life. I'm able to say I am healed by the blood of Christ. I am a new creation because of Christ's death on the cross for ALL of my sins.

Before I go out, I go over this checklist to ensure that I don't end up doing something stupid.

- **Who** am I going out with? Are they going to hinder or sabotage my sobriety?
- **What** am I going to be doing? Is the event or activity that I'm attending going to go against what I know is right?
- **When** am I coming home? The later I stay out, the more likely I will be to screw up.
- **Why** am I going? Are the motives pure or are they because I want an excuse to party?
- **How** am I going to stay sober if temptation comes my way? If I know that the who, what, when, or why are going to be in conflict with my goals—this is the most important factor—how will I go home sober?

When making any decisions, I base it on HALT. I will never decide what to do or say when I am **H**ungry, **A**ngry, **L**onely, or **T**ired.

And last but not least, how do I live a joyful life? **J**esus first; **O**thers second; **Y**ourself last.

If I get my strength through Christ then there is nothing I cannot accomplish. If I think of others before my own selfish desires, I will be less likely to do something stupid. If I put myself last, I will doing exactly what Jesus did when He died on the cross.

Grace is free of charge, no strings attached, on the house. (*What's So Amazing About Grace?* by Peter Yancey) It's simple yet difficult. Simple because all it takes is having faith in God; difficult because it believes in something you cannot see. Walking the narrow path leads to real living. While following what the world does is easy, it leads to a life of short-term satisfaction but eternal misery. Just remember that Satan is the one who condemns us; God convicts us. Chase those dreams, and don't let Satan's lies continue to hold you from your destiny of success.

How can others get clean? You need to want it. Realize that without God you can't do it. For those who say Christianity is a crutch… it is. But on our own we cannot stand! The moment you accept that you need help is the moment you begin recovery. You need to have your own faith—not a parent's, sibling's, or friend's. Your faith needs to be your own because only a personal relationship with Christ will lead to victory.

Grace   July 16th, 2008

"For we know that our old self was crucified with Him so that the body of sin might be done away with, that we should no longer be slaves to sin." Romans 6:6

When I was still out in the world partying it up and causing chaos, I always had this guilt that my sins were so bad I could never be forgiven. Ultimately, that was just Satan playing tricks on me because the scripture clearly states that because of Christ's death on the cross, ALL my sins are forgiven.

If you are struggling with guilt and remorse, give it to God. When you can let go of your past is when you can finally move forward in life. God doesn't want us to come to Him when we are perfect and have our lives totally together; He wants to help us! He has promised us so much in life. An abundant and joyful life is only a prayer away.

Don't dwell on the past; live for today. And when thinking of what you want to do in the future, picture that Christ is right next to you. In fact, Christ is always walking next to us, holding our hand through the darkest times, hugging us and giving us love when we are hurt and sad. Our Savior is an almighty God who knows what we need.

He loves us so much that He doesn't force His way into our hearts; He gives us choices. His love eventually leads us to His grace. "Grace doesn't depend on suffering to exist, but where there is suffering there is God's grace." (*The Shack* by William P. Young)

"He mocks proud mockers, but gives grace to the humble." Proverbs 3:33

Another Lesson in Life   July 18th, 2008

Tonight I realized that I'm a different person. The sights, sounds, and environments that used to energize me now drain me. I see how I used to act and interact in any situation. That person was just a show, a facade that really wasn't me. I now dread being in a nightclub scene; being around drunk and obnoxious people takes too much energy. I always thought I could handle any situation; I was wrong. Maybe who I am with factors into the equation.

Coming to grips with who I am today, away from the comforts of home, is a stark reminder of how far I've come. Walking out of a crowded place, uneasy and uncomfortable, is a sobering reminder. For the first time I actually thought about a drink; it would loosen me up and make me more sociable. In the end, reality set in and, if that's what I need to do to fit in, then that's not who I am.

It sucks that I fooled myself for so long thinking that I could be a normal person when what I am is a recovering alcoholic. I'm unable to be in certain environments (bars, nightclubs, etc). Who I am is someone that has had a total transformation.

How I tested the limits were dumb. It was an act that, had it not been for Christ's strength to walk out, who knows what would have happened. The reason I'm in Laguna, away from the party scene in LA, is simple: God knows that that's no longer who I am.

Live by the Spirit   July 18th, 2008

"So I say, live by the Spirit, and you will not gratify the desires of the sinful nature. For the sinful nature desires what is contrary to the Spirit, and the Spirit what is contrary to the sinful nature. They are in conflict with each other, so that you do not do what you want. But if you are led by the Spirit, you are not under law. The acts of the sinful nature are obvious: sexual immorality, impurity and debauchery; idolatry and witchcraft; hatred, discord, jealousy, fits of rage, selfish ambition, dissensions, factions and envy; drunkenness, orgies, and the like. I warn you, as I did before, that those who live like this will not inherit the kingdom of God. But the fruit of the Spirit is love, joy, peace, patience, kindness, goodness, faithfulness, gentleness, and self-control. Against such things there is no law. Those who belong to Christ Jesus have crucified the sinful nature with its passions and desires. Since we live by the Spirit, let us keep in step with the Spirit. Let us not become conceited, provoking and envying each other."
Galatians 5:16-25

It's so awesome how simply the Bible explains life. The good, the bad, and the ugly can all be summed up in this passage of scripture. Despite all my shortcomings, Christ's love covers my transgressions. I like to think of God's Word not as rules but as guidelines that enable me to live a joyful life.

For so many years I exemplified verses 19-21. They explain how sinful and evil I really was. I refer to these characteristics as the "poison" of life. The great part is that verses 22-24 show how, despite all my failures, He still loved me. The Fruit of the Spirit clearly states that forgiveness is a key component.

If I'm to forgive others then it's a given that God has forgiven me. I live each day making decisions based on these qualities. If the action or result doesn't line up with the Fruit of the Spirit, I know that I'm doing something wrong. Ephesians 5:18 says to "be filled with the Spirit." This word "filled" is a command. All believers are to be filled with the Spirit which should lead to the Fruit of the Spirit.

I find it amazing that it starts with love and ends with self-control. These two Fruits were the most difficult for me. Besides not loving others or even myself, I couldn't love God. I couldn't give to others what Jesus gives to me unconditionally. Because of my rebellion and anger, I ultimately had no self-control, unable to control what I put into my body and incapable of being a man of God. Now that my personal walk with Christ is in order, I'm able to love again, and I'm able to control my desires and serve the Lord.

Prayer Request   July 18th, 2008

I have all these hopes and dreams. The vision I have is so huge that at times I feel overwhelmed. On my own, I have no chance of accomplishing it. For those of you who pray…I need it. Pray that I do exactly what I'm supposed to do; that I hear what God has planned for me; that when doors are closed, I accept it; that when doors are opened, I walk through them. I know in my heart that God has amazing things planned, but I have to step out in faith. The uncertainty is scary. You have all played a very important role in my life, and today I'm asking that you help me even more by praying that I would follow God's will without hesitation and that I would be able to discern His plan for my life. Thanks.

Love   July 18th, 2008

"Love bears all things, believes all things, hopes all things, endures all things." 1 Corinthians 13:7

Love has no limits. Do those closest to you know that they can fail and do foolish things and yet you will love them? Love assumes the best about others. Never lose hope in the ones you love. Practice the same unconditional love towards others that Christ gives to you.

As I continue to seek God, He continues to show me how inadequate I really am. However, with His guidance and love, anything is possible. Instead of focusing on love as the world sees it, I'm beginning to comprehend that TRUE love isn't an emotion or a feeling; true love is an act.

Love is mostly a foreign concept to me. In fact, only now do I think I even have the capacity to love someone other than myself. For so many years I've put Jon before everything. The love God has for us was clearly shown when His only Son was sent to die on the cross. There is the saying, "WWJD (What Would Jesus Do?)" Maybe it's time to change it to WWID. What Will I Do?

Insight   July 18th, 2008

by Clifford Park, D.D.S.

Hi Jon,

Didn't get a chance to talk to you the last time you brought your grandmother in to the office. How has your schedule been so far at Laguna Beach? The sad fact is that way too many people you see every week in church struggle with some sort of addiction. You were the only one honest enough to share your struggles with alcohol. A friend whom I've known since my undergrad days in Seattle recently died from a massive heart attack. The cause? Believe it or not, it all started from envy and jealousy that drove him to living a lifestyle way beyond reasonable. Even though a Christian, he was very private and reserved when it came to talking about spiritual matters, and he generally put up a wall when that subject was brought up. He was very funny and a great conversationalist that I really enjoyed being around. But beneath all that was a very frustrated and unhappy person.

I think another important key to maintaining one's walk with God is [having] at least one person you can confide in and share your deep struggles with. All of my close spiritual friends are on the mainland, and those guys played a key role in my not being way out in left field. A guy who was influential spiritually early on when I was an undergrad says, "You got to trust in God, not in man." I guess that's the challenge—to not place your trust in another person; God has to be your ultimate source of joy and security. Drop a line when you can and let me know how things are going.

Blessings to you,
Cliff

Insight from a Parent   July 19th, 2008

I've asked my family members to give words of wisdom for the family and friends of those struggling with addiction.

By: Glenn (Jon's Dad)

Don't be afraid of the truth; the truth will set you free. I was afraid of the truth that my son was addicted so every denial and every time he pointed the finger at someone else was a relief. But the truth was that I didn't want to know. Eventually the truth came out, and by God's mercy, it wasn't too late. Be careful what you wish for; sometimes you get what you wish for. If you wish that there is no problem, you probably will get your wish, sort of.

I'm Not Alone   July 21st, 2008

"Therefore, since we are surrounded by such a great cloud of witnesses, let us throw off everything that hinders and the sin that so easily entangles, and let us run with perseverance the race marked out for us. Let us fix our eyes on Jesus, the author and perfecter of our faith, who for the joy set before him endured the cross, scorning its shame, and sat down at the right hand of the throne of God. Consider him who endured such opposition from sinful men, so that you will not grow weary and lose heart." Hebrews 12:1-3

When I first got sober I had no clue what to do. I was sent to a rehab center across the ocean. No cell phone, limited times to call home, no friends...I had nothing. At least that's what Satan wanted me to believe. When I turned to Christ, I realized that I wasn't alone...I had Jesus.

I've had this problem of getting easily distracted and unable to finish what I start. Luckily, I've kept my eyes on the prize. It wasn't only about sobriety or changing who I was; it was focusing on restoring my relationship with Christ. It's a process that continues daily as I search for His wisdom and guidance. I don't spend my time dwelling on what's going on around me; I do what verse two says: I fix my eyes on Jesus.

My life isn't easier than it once was. Actually, moving back to California is difficult. If I were to think as the world thinks, it would depress me. Once again I'm far from home; very few close friends; all the challenges of starting over; clueless to where to eat, where to shop, etc. However, if I look at things from a supernatural perspective, I have so much to be grateful for; I have so many people praying for me; and I realize that as long as I focus on searching for a better relationship with Christ, everything will be okay. Wait—not okay; everything will be awesome.

No Fear   July 22nd, 2008

Today I was asked to speak at my old rehab center. For whatever reason, every time I go there to share, I get a little nervous. Usually preparing for a speech is easy and doesn't require much thought. I guess since this was where I first began my sobriety, there's a little more pressure.

As usual, I sent out requests for prayer before I was to speak. The response from those I texted was amazing. It never ceases to amaze me how many wonderful and supportive people I have in my life. The replies all basically said the same thing—don't worry; you'll do fine.

Two minutes before I was to speak, my friend Tabol sent this message: "Be a lion. Proverbs 28." At that point I was actually debating how in-depth I was going to go about my walk with Christ. The other panel members had multiple years of sobriety and were die-hard 12-Step guys. Part of me was a little intimidated because I didn't know how they would react. Encouraged by Tabol's message, I didn't change a thing in my presentation and focused on living a joyful life with Christ as the source of strength.

The people I was sharing with nodded in agreement, but the coolest part was seeing the 12-Step guys agreeing also. In fact, at the end of the night, the leader who coordinates numerous talks asked me if I'd be interested in joining their group. He said it was a breath of fresh air to hear my view on sobriety and that he thinks it would be good to have me share more often. Despite my growth over the last year, I was actually hesitant to be a "lion" for Christ today. I was once again reminded how powerful prayer can be. The simple task of asking others for prayer allowed me to touch the lives of others tonight and enabled me to stand firm in my belief that it's only through Christ that one can live a life of joy.

I also have a few names to add to the prayer list…Casey, JB, Chris, Scotty, Rich, Brandon, and Greg. I find it fascinating that it seems every day God places someone new in my life that's in need of prayer.

Peace   *July 23rd, 2008*

"I'm leaving you peace. I'm giving you my peace. I don't give you the kind of peace that the world gives. So don't be troubled or cowardly." John 14:27

Applying this verse today is difficult. I'm across the ocean and hearing that my family back home is going through some rough times. My grandmother's not doing so well and is causing some major headaches. She's not exactly "all there". She locked herself out of the house, pressed her Life Alert, and when there was no response, they thought she had died. Everything is okay; she was just so confused and couldn't figure out how to open the door.

On top of that, with the economy the way it is, our family business is going through some changes and my mom is under a lot of pressure. The salon has been around for over 45 years, and for 13 years was a vital part of my life. Knowing things aren't running smoothly is difficult for me to bear.

Despite all the positive things that have been going on here on the mainland, my immediate thought was that I needed to go home and help out the family and fix things. Maybe my friend Kelsie was right when she said I'm a control freak. The fact of the matter is that I can't fix it; only God can.

As I sit here in a large, empty room knowing how difficult life is for my family back home, still I'm at peace. For so long I disobeyed God and did things my way. However, the moment I turn things over to His care is the moment I find peace even when things are rough. It's easy to be at peace when things are going well; it's a whole different story to have peace when life is turned upside down.

Finally   *July 24th, 2008*

Place in this World by Michael W. Smith

The wind is moving
But I am standing still
A life of pages
Waiting to be filled
A heart that's hopeful
A head that's full of dreams
But this becoming
Is harder than it seems
Feels like I'm

Chorus:
Looking for a reason
Roaming through the night to find
My place in this world
My place in this world
Not a lot to lean on
I need your light to help me find
My place in this world
My place in this world

If there are millions
Down on their knees
Among the many
Can you still hear me
Hear me asking
Where do I belong
Is there a vision
That I can call my own
Show me

    This used to be one of my favorite songs. I remember singing this in the car all the time, never realizing how much it would impact my life. For so many years I just wandered through life doing whatever I wanted. Even though I worked for the family business and thought my heart was in it, in reality I was just fooling myself.

    With lots of idle time, I ended up going down the wrong path. Despite the appearance of being happy where I was in life, I was miserable. Deep within my soul, I was still searching for a reason to live. Although I've been in California for three weeks, I still have doubts that this is where I'm supposed to be.

Tonight I got my answer: this is my place in the world for now. On Wednesday nights, I lead a Bible study for addicts. Even though I've had years of training and parents who were amazing Sunday School teachers, I had this fear that I would never be effective as a Bible teacher. When it came time for prayer requests, I mentioned that I was homesick and was wondering if this is where I was supposed to be.

When I was driving home, I got a voice mail from Tammy. She was crying and saying that what I was teaching had been very helpful—that she learns so much whenever I teach. Hearing her say how I'm a blessing to her life made me want to cry. A little over a year removed from living a life of sin, and now God is using me to touch the lives of others. Simply amazing.

Living in California may be for only two years, but for the first time in my life, I know where I belong. I've finally found my place in this world.

The Right Source   July 28th, 2008

"It is God who arms me with strength and makes my way perfect." 2 Samuel 22:23

Wow, this past weekend has been an eye opener. On Friday I was in a meeting and a very large, angry guy just totally went off. He was angry about numerous things, yelling and saying things that scared most of the people there. Maybe he didn't express it in the right way but deep down he was hurt. He was going to be a godfather to his cousin's baby but the baby was stillborn.

He wanted to drink, beat people up, and go back to his gang lifestyle. He wanted to take out all the frustration but was unable to let those feelings show in a positive way. After exploding on the group, he just left. While some people commented and were being sarcastic concerning what he had shared, I thought what he said was real.

I couldn't handle the negativity that was in the room so I went out to get some fresh air. While I was outside I saw him walking back, mad as hell. For whatever reason, I had this feeling that I was supposed to talk to him—a 6-foot, 250-pound, pissed off, gang member who looked like he was going to kill someone.

I'd never met this guy before. Common sense would have been to leave him alone. However, I went up to him, shook his hand, and told him thanks for sharing. He stared at me with eyes that scared me. I let him know how it had affected me and that I appreciated his being real about his emotions. After that, his expression softened and eventually we had a deep conversation.

In the end, we prayed together and really got to know each other. I ended up driving him home, and we talked some more. The bottom line is that he didn't go out and do anything stupid. He's still sober today. And as for me, I learned that when you're following the will of God and allowing Him to be in control, fear isn't an option because He will give the strength to overcome all things.

Doing Things the Right Way   July 29th, 2008

Over the last three days I was at a soccer tournament watching teams from Hawaii compete against teams from all over the United States. Throughout the tourney I witnessed dirty play and horrendous behavior of parents from the other teams and horrible officiating. Through it all the Hawaii boys maintained their composure and remained absolute gentlemen.

While observing other games there were fights, coaches being ejected, and even a parent being barred from watching the game.

Overall it was a poor display of sportsmanship. Luckily, the Hawaii team made it to the championship game despite the odds having been stacked against them.

It was an absolutely GREAT game even though they lost. In reality, they were total winners in my eyes. They were heroes for playing the game the right way. They didn't cheat, maintained their dignity, and were true champions in the sense that they didn't conform to the circumstances in order to win.

For so many years of my life I was always about results. I just wanted to come out on top. I would take shortcuts, lie, cheat, and steal. While I may have achieved my goals, I could never look in the mirror and not have regrets. I've come to see that life is a process, the things you do and the things you say will ultimately determine if you can look in the mirror and say you did it the right way.

Today was a simple reminder that it's not about winning or losing; it's how you play the game. If you win in disgrace, no one will remember who you are or will for all the wrong reasons. But if you come up short while never sacrificing morals or dignity, you will never be forgotten. HSC Bulls 2008, you did it the right way.

Fighting addictions is never easy; it's a battle that will be waged for the rest of my life. The moment I take shortcuts, the day I try and cheat, that instance when I lie to myself about what I'm doing is a day I never want to see. The only way to living a joyful and honest life is doing things the right way.

<u>In Christ Alone</u>   <u>July 30th, 2008</u>

In Christ Alone by Michael English. Wow, what a powerful song. Usually when I speak in churches I often reference this song.

The first time I heard it after rehab, I cried like a baby—so much that I had to pull over on the side of the road to compose myself.

No matter if it's in my success or failures, everything is for the glory of God. When I fail, it's by His grace that I can get back on my feet and start again. Whenever I do things right, it's because He gives me the strength to succeed. There are so many lines from the song that have meaning to me, but the two verses that speak to me the most are:

For only by His grace
I am redeemed
And only His tender mercy
Could reach beyond my weakness
To my need

This was the part of the song that made me bawl my eyes out. On my own I am a weak human being—unable to control my urges and an absolute train wreck. However, since Jesus sacrificed His life on the cross, all my sins are forgiven. He suffered all the pain and heartache for me. Because of that I am redeemed; I am able to live a life that can be a light for others.

Only through the grace of God am I alive today. Regardless of how difficult life is, as long as I place my trust in an awesome God, everything will be amazing.

And in every victory
Let it be said of me
My source of strength
My source of hope
Is Christ alone.

I've had many people ask me how I got sober—how I no longer have the urge to do drugs and alcohol when so many fail to overcome—how I went from a nightclubbing, drug abusing, drunk, self-centered, egomaniac that almost killed himself from years of abuse to a man who has an overwhelming desire to help others battle addiction. The answer is the chorus above.

Without my personal relationship with Christ, I would never have changed. He gives me my strength and my hope. For those who don't understand how can you trust in something you cannot see, it's a simple thing called faith. It's accepting that something bigger and better than ourselves is in control. My "higher power" is Jesus Christ.

When I was in control of my life, I was a mess. Looking back, a stronger thing was in control of my life: Satan. There is good vs. evil. And the evil one who is out to destroy was decimating my life. The day I turned my life back over to Christ was the day that I regained love, joy, peace, patience, kindness, goodness, faithfulness, humility, and self-control.

Behind the Scenes   July 31st, 2008

The last couple of days I was stressing out because I was under the impression that I had to have a degree in order to get my CADC (Certified Alcohol & Drug Counselor) certification. I was frustrated that the information I had thought valid, wasn't. I was beating myself up that I hadn't researched it enough and placed my trust in the wrong people. My original plan was shot and I didn't want to face reality.

Last night I just decided not to stress about it, taking the attitude that whatever happens, happens. When I woke up this morning, I went to my old rehab and asked more questions. Come to find out, even though 84% of those with CADC have a college degree, it wasn't necessary to acquire the certification; it just helps when applying for a job.

I'm blessed that I have three rehabs that are willing to help me gain the required hours for certification. I'm blessed that despite lacking the degree I've been fortunate enough to connect with the right people who will assist me in accomplishing my dream. Another cool part was that one of my friends who is attempting to get her Ph.D. took time out of her busy schedule to write out an action plan for me. It was nice to have her outlook on things and an alternative plan of action to accomplish my goals.

For the past year I've been reading devotionals by Joel Osteen. Like him or not, one of the main things I kept reading was that God is always working behind the scenes in my favor. Over the last 24 hours I've realized that He has been working behind the scenes lining up the right people at the right time to help me along the way.

The whole time I've been speaking and sharing my testimony, I never did it for personal gain or money. However, the Lord has rewarded me for my service and willingness to help others. He's placed in my life people who are able to help me in ways that money cannot, people who care and are willing to go the extra mile for me.

Whenever I question to what lengths I would go to help others, I have a song that comes to mind:

Make me a servant
Humble and meek
Lord may I lift up
Those who are weak
Now may the prayer of my heart always be
Make me a servant

It's kind of funny that the whole time I was using that song to help me be willing to help others, God was finding others to help *me* when I was weak.

Work for God   August 1st, 2008

Last night I was having another bout of insomnia. I happened across a sermon by Dr. Charles Stanley. When I was younger, my family would visit his church each time we were on the East coast. Our library at home probably has every single book he's ever written along with hundreds of tapes and CDs by In Touch Ministries.

His messages are just like I remembered them—to the point, entertaining, and most of all, full of truths that can be used daily. The key points were that we need to serve God regardless of our age and that we need to pray for others. Most importantly, we are to be messengers of God's amazing love.

It seems that I have good days and bad days concerning why I'm in California—setbacks and successes which lead to feelings of doubt vs. confidence, moments of unbelievable clarity and days it seems my brain just isn't working. Dr. Stanley reminded me that if I really want to serve God, I just need to do it and have Christ as my focus.

If I'm selfish, self-centered, and have continuing sin in my life, it will be a hindrance to serving God; however, if I'm available, humble, and my motivation is pure, then God can do great things. When God is behind you, anything can happen. If you look at some of the most influential people in the Bible, they were men and women who had committed murders, adultery, denied Christ, were unscrupulous tax collectors, etc.

Most telling is that some of the twelve disciples who ultimately started the church were uneducated fisherman. When God calls and you answer, spectacular events will follow. He wants to use us for the rest of our lives to share the awesome gift of salvation. If there is ever a purpose or direction in life, work for Jesus.

"The righteous will flourish like a palm tree; they will grow like a cedar of Lebanon planted in the house of the LORD; they will flourish in the courts of our God. They will still bear fruit in old age; they will stay fresh and green." Psalm 92:12-14

Faith...Ephesians 2:8   August 2nd, 2008

"For it is by grace you have been saved, through faith—and this not from yourselves, it is the gift of God." Ephesians 2:8

I have a tattoo on my leg—the kanji for faith with Ephesians 2:8, a simple reminder that it's not anything that I've done that has spared me from suffering the pain of addiction. It's only by the grace of God that He has healed me, and due, in part, to my faith.

The first night that I was in rehab, I was scared—20 guys absolutely struggling with addictions. The person who came to welcome me was a little on the eccentric side. The fear that overcame me was enormous. I'd heard that for some, it was their tenth time in rehab. There was no way I wanted to put my family through 10 times of sending me away.

Before I went to sleep I got on my knees and prayed, "God, if I'm going to struggle with addiction for the rest of my life, I don't want to wake up. However, if I do wake up, I will know that I'm healed and will dedicate the rest of my life to helping those struggling with addiction." The next morning, the only reminder I had of my struggle was a stuffy nose.

This isn't to say that I don't have difficult days. I'm blessed that those rare weak moments only last for a moment. I have an absolute faith that I am healed. Some say it's a mental thing, that the reason I'm sober is because I wanted it. That is partially true; it's just missing where my source of strength comes from. The 12-Step Program has a saying that it's only through a higher power that one can be relieved. It's true, and my "higher power" is Christ.

Over the last month in California I've come across hundreds of people suffering from addictions. The one thing I've learned is that I'm really, really fortunate to be in the position I am today. I hear all types of stories concerning how people are struggling. Deep down inside I just want to yell, "Put your faith in Christ! It's not a thing you do once in a while; it's not a passing feeling. It's a way of life."

Sometimes I wonder why I'm so blessed. Then I remember that it's not just one thing. It's personal prayer, prayer from others, a personal relationship with Christ, reading the Bible, helping others, being positive, and most importantly, having faith that God is in control. Faith isn't just standing around and doing nothing. Faith, according to Webster's Dictionary is "allegiance to duty or a person." That means doing what God has told me to do.

My Dad   August 3rd, 2008

Today was spent watching the Hall of Fame induction ceremony for the National Football League. I heard sons saying how great their dads were and how they had influenced who they are. It got me to thinking that even though my father has never played a professional game in his life, he's my Hall of Fame Dad.

If I was inducting my Dad into the Hall of Fame, this is what I would say…

My dad is the most influential man in my life. When I was a child, he'd take me fishing every Saturday morning. We'd be up before the sun came up, driving to Sandy Beach for a few hours of bonding. Unfortunately, my sister Marissa would sometimes come and cut short our outing. She liked to eat the bread that was used as bait. He could have been golfing, fishing on a boat, or sleeping in because of a long, hard work week. But no matter what, his kids always came first.

Dad was also there for all my sporting events—never missed a game; and for that matter, never missed a practice. While other kids would be waiting to be picked up, Dad was never more that few feet away. It didn't matter if my team didn't win a game the whole season or if we went undefeated (I was on both), his support and dedication never wavered.

As I grew older and decided baseball and basketball wasn't the thing for me, he didn't freak out or force me to go back. Instead he supported my new passion…body boarding. He would come down to the beach and be the only parent taking pictures of his son. When I was old enough to drive and go down by myself, he allowed me the freedom to grow into adulthood.

Like many father-son relationships, we grew apart during my teenage years yet Dad worked at finding common ground, whether it be computers, UH football games, or the Dallas Cowboys. He always found something we could have a conversation about. While some of my friends complained about their dads, I really couldn't say much. As dorky as he was, he was still pretty cool.

When my mom got sick, our family could've totally fallen apart. It was Dad's strength and walk with the Lord that was our glue. I don't think it was until Mom was in ICU and close to death that I finally saw him cry. This was almost seven years after her initial diagnosis. It was at this point that I realized how special my dad is.

Around that time I was involved with some shady things. The men I was associating with had mistresses and were in the bar every night while their wives were at home with the kids. Here was my dad, married to the same woman for over 20 years, her health deteriorating, and he was still by her side. I'll never forget what my dad said when I asked him why he was crying: "I'm afraid I'll lose my best friend."

For the next couple of years I really took a turn for the worse—numerous fights with constant yelling, accusations, and bickering; and in the end, threats of how I would be disowned. Luckily, Dad never gave up on me. He loved me unconditionally.

I'll never forget the day before I admitted to my parents that I needed help. Dad pulled me into the office and asked me if everything was okay. He told me that no matter what was going on, he still loved me. He prayed with tears streaming down his face yet I lied and denied that anything was wrong. However, that prayer and talk tugged at my heart until a few hours later when I finally admitted what I was doing. Dad saved my life.

My dad may not be the richest man on the earth. He may never find the cure for cancer. He will never win a championship in any sport. Heck, he will never be the coolest guy in the room. But today I can say that my Dad is my best friend. He has set the standard for what it is to be a son, husband, and most importantly, a father. He is someone I look up to. He is the one person I call when I need some deep and honest advice. He is my Dad.

<u>Mom</u>   <u>August 4th, 2008</u>

Today was baby dedication day at church. I realized that this was what Mom had done before my sister and I were born. Her prayer was simple: if we were not going to be servants of His, she didn't want any kids.

Maybe it was because of this prayer that my mom never gave up on me. She was always the one who would save my butt when my dad and I fought. As horrible and evil as I turned out to be, she never stopped calling to tell me to watch a certain pastor. I will admit that I'm a spoiled mama's boy. Why not? Mom has always supported me.

I'm still not at the point in my life where sharing about my mother's illness will be open and totally honest. Her sickness has affected our family, and even as I write this now, I still get choked up.

It's been a struggle seeing a once vibrant woman who has touched so many lives still battling her disease. I often questioned God as to why He had allowed her to get sick. Why would He take my mom away from me? Why would He allow my family to go through the hell of seeing her this way? I still haven't gotten an answer; in fact, I've just come to the conclusion that it doesn't matter anymore. The bottom line is that God knows best and I still have her in my life.

When I look back and see what she's gone through, I have learned so much. First, my mom is a fighter. Despite her laid-back attitude towards most things, she is fighting to be there for my dad, my sister, and myself. She has fought back against all odds. When in the ICU, her chances of survival were really slim. My girlfriend at the time was in the medical field and didn't have the heart to tell me that my mom was moments away from death. She told me that my mom's recovery had been a miracle.

Mom never gives up and never gives in. She will fight for what's right. If there's an injustice, she will stand up even if it means she has to do it alone. She's showed me that you fight for the right things; and in her case, she fights for her family all the time.

The second thing I realized about my mom is that she puts others before herself. My dad has shared that mom takes all these experimental treatments just so she can be there for Marissa and me. She could do less damage to her body with other treatments, but she wouldn't be able to do as much. She chose to risk further damage so she could be as much of a mom as she can be for us.

I remember that when Marissa was about to get married, Mom did everything a normal / healthy person would do—all the bridal showers, planning, and shopping...plus having to send her addict son to rehab. Looking back, she gave every ounce of strength and more.

The third thing I've come to see is her servant's heart. Even though the illness has her so tired she's sometimes sleeping at 1 p.m., if anyone is sick, she'll cook for them. If someone is in the hospital, she'll visit them. If someone needs a ride to the supermarket, she'll drive. My mom is a selfless servant who exemplifies Christ-like love.

I remember 20 years ago when the AIDS virus was first appearing on the scene. We had a worker who eventually died from it. At that time there was very little information concerning the disease. Despite the unfounded warning from others, Mom was always there for Daniel. She never treated him any differently. She was a friend 'til the end. What I learned from her was something I'll never forget: treat everyone the same.

I don't know if Mom will ever be the same person physically as she was 14 years ago. The one thing I do know is that the person she is today is someone I would never trade in a trillion years. Her illness has been hard, but it has made our family stronger; it's made us think more of others, strive to be more servant-like, and most importantly, it's made me realize that having a heart of gold is priceless.

Her tears are because she can feel the Holy Spirit's presence a little more keenly than others. Her source of strength to be a fighter and her compassion for the less fortunate come from Christ. For so long I hated God for what He had allowed to happen to Mom. I even held resentment towards her for being sick. Today I realize I was an idiot. My mom has taught me so much about following Christ when times are tough. She has exemplified living a life dedicated to God.

If I could take only one quality from Mom, it would be her heart. Why? Because she has a heart of gold. I used to tease my mom all the time when she would just start crying in church or at a movie. I've come to see that's because she has a soft spot for everyone. Amazingly, because of her illness she's in love with God even more.

My Past   August 6th, 2008

As I was working out at 24-Hour Fitness, I had my iPod on shuffle and was stopped dead in my tracks when *Lifelong Vacation* by Paul De Lea came on. It is a Progressive House song so I really do not expect anyone to know it, but it was one of my favorite songs for about a year. A good portion of my druggy days was spent at the The Living Room, and this was the last song played almost every night for six months.

Tonight it brought back a flood of memories about my hard partying days. The crazy late nights that lasted until 10…in the morning, the ridiculous amounts of Jack Daniels that I drank, and the insane volume of ecstasy which I took that eventually led to my highly addictive cocaine love affair. I've never really shared about how bad my addictions once were or the depths of debauchery to which I traveled.

I try to forget about my past and focus on the present, but someone once said that in order for people to understand how far I've come, they need to know how low I went. For 13 years of my life, I was one screwed-up guy. I dealt drugs, worked at gambling rooms, took and placed bets for football, was a daily patron at basically every single "cool" bar on the island. I've seen and done things that I'm definitely not proud of.

I've consumed alcohol to the point that I would black out and wake up on the bathroom floor. The amount of drugs I did is mind-boggling. I would take everything that was available. The only drug I've not tried is heroin, and that's because I'm afraid of needles. I lost over $10,000 in a single weekend of gambling before I even turned 21. At one time, I was the manager of a gambling room. Of the eight workers, only two of us have not been in jail. What I'm trying to get at is that from where I was to where I am is a miracle. I'm not proud of my past, but it has made me who I am today.

No human could have put my life back in order. No organization or motivational speaker would have been able to get me back on the right path. What I do know that has helped was a ton of prayer from friends and family. Having people in my life who were willing to have "sober fun" with me was also a huge bonus. However, the biggest asset in my newly found life was, and still is, my personal relationship with Christ.

It's only through Him that all my sins are forgiven. For a long time I carried this guilt about all the evil things I once did. The guilt fed my depression and the feeling that I could never be forgiven. This just gave me another excuse to party and to continue in a life of sin. Today all of that is a thing of the past. Today I live a life of hope, a life that is once again driven by goals and dreams.

Emotions   August 7th, 2008

The two-year-old that is part of the family I'm living with is pretty sick, and it has really affected me. It's been a while since I genuinely cared for someone new. This little kid has definitely found a place in my heart.

Seeing him in the hospital was a difficult thing; it brought back memories of visiting my grandfathers before they passed away. The funny thing is that for the longest time I had this aversion to going to hospitals. Maybe it's because I've finally been able to deal with my emotions that I was able to visit Alex today.

It's been 15 months since I got sober, and over time I've come to terms with understanding my feelings. I'm just now starting to be able to love someone other than family and friends. It's amazing that this little guy has cracked my thick shell of a heart. Every day I can count on hearing him say, "I love you, Jonny." His grandma shared that when he goes through his list of people he loves, I'm included.

For the last couple of days we've been draining the infection, and my job was to hold him down while they squeezed the puss out. It was heart wrenching to hear him scream and ask me why I wouldn't let him go. Totally sucks to have a two-year-old ask why you are hurting him. When they took him to the ER, they found a cyst in his leg and we were told that luckily it hadn't burst.

If it had, he would possibly have lost his leg. The doctors are now saying that if the staph infection has spread to the bone, they will have to do major surgery.

If you love someone, let him or her know. You never know when or if you will have a chance to say it again. I also learned that feelings are okay to have. Even if I'm sad about what's going on, I now realize that I'm no longer emotionally void. Just because I'm sober doesn't mean that life is going to get any easier. What it does mean is that I'm better able to handle situations, good or bad.

Please keep Alexander in your prayers. He's a tough little kid, but nonetheless, very sick and fighting as best he can.

A Great Weekend   August 11th, 2008

I had an absolutely great weekend from the Pageant of Masters Arts Festival to the John Heffron Comedy Central Taping (3rd row center) to an afternoon at California Adventure Park—fun times with some really terrific people. I think this was the most fun I've had in a long time. I learned that I could go to and do activities like I used to; it's only a matter of who I spend my time with.

Saturday night I was surrounded by wine booths and a comedy club where it seemed everyone was drinking. Back home it was always "safe" to go out because the venues I visited had bartenders and waitresses who knew I'd been to rehab and was turning over a new leaf. Interestingly, the ones who used to serve me the most were the very ones who most supported my decision to be sober.

Tara and Eddie didn't have to "babysit", or should I say "sobersit", because we just had a blast hanging out and talking and alcohol had not even been a thought. I was also fortunate enough to meet some of Tara's friends at the comedy event and we got along great. In one of my earlier posts I wrote about not being as outgoing as I once was. I was wrong.

Today I was lucky to spend time with Jaclyn at the California Adventure Park. It was nice to see someone from home and just hang out. We didn't go on too many rides; we just talked and laughed and talked some more. It was as if we'd never been apart. We agreed that we would rather have been at Shokudo (our favorite and most frequented restaurant back home) for dinner but were just glad to be together.

Overall, this weekend had to have been one of the best since I've been in California: great people, events, and memories. If I have any advice to give to anyone newly sober or struggling with enjoying life in sobriety, it's this: surround yourself with people who will support your decision. I've been blessed this weekend with a reminder that being sober doesn't mean staying in a room and doing nothing; it's about living a joyful life and living life to the fullest.

Who Am I?   August 12th, 2008

Who Am I by Casting Crowns

Who am I?
That the Lord of all the earth
Would care to know my name,
Would care to feel my hurt.

Who am I?
That the bright and morning star
Would choose to light the way
For my ever wandering heart.

Who am I?
That the eyes that see my sin
Would look on me with love
And watch me rise again.

Who am I?
That the voice that calmed the sea
Would call out through the rain
And calm the storm in me.

Not because of who I am,
But because of what you've done.
Not because of what I've done,
But because of who you are.

I am a flower quickly fading,
Here today and gone tomorrow,
A wave tossed in the ocean,
A vapor in the wind.
Still you hear me when I'm calling,
Lord, you catch me when I'm falling,
And you've told me who I am.
I am yours.

Sobriety is a gift from God. It's something I could never do on my own, a blessing for which I will be forever grateful. I sometimes ponder why I am the one out of my group that is still sober. I wonder even more why I've been able to live such a wonderful and joyful life while I see others with much more time just living day to day. When I heard this song, I had my answer. It's nothing about me; it's all about my source of strength.

For many years I went through life on my own. Every accomplishment and every failure was mine alone. That way of living eventually led me to be a self-centered, raging alcoholic with a major drug addiction. Many nights I would run from my problems by drinking a bottle of Jack Daniels or consuming copious amounts of drugs. The whole time I had a loving and powerful God just waiting for me to ask Him for help. Stupid is the only term to describe it.

It didn't matter how far I ran from my faith nor did it matter how severe my addictions were or how stupid I became. Jesus' death on the cross made it possible for me to come back to Him. Not only was I forgiven, but I was able to have a peace in my life that I had forgotten existed.

When battling addictions, I felt that I was all alone. There was no longer any hope in living life. It is a depressing state of mind that had trapped me in a never-ending cycle of self-loathing and self-destruction. I believed I had done too many horrible things to ever be made clean. If I was to have redemption through a human, I would be sent to hell. However, because my redemption is from Christ, I was given a second chance.

Thank You   *August 13th, 2008*

When I was in treatment, one of the workers got pissed off at us and said we would all relapse—that out of 100, only two stay sober for a year, and after that, only 1 out of 100 will make it to year two. I used those statistics as motivation; it seems that others used it as an excuse to fail.

I bring this up because I want to talk for a minute about motivation. I've always viewed challenges as a way to test myself. If someone said I couldn't do something, I would do whatever it took to accomplish it. That drive and determination has helped me overcome all the obstacles that have come my way. In no way do I take the credit; I've had a lot of help along the way.

I want to take the time today to thank all those who have been helpful throughout this season of my life. First, I want to thank my family. It was hard for them to deal with my addictions. Through constant prayer and words of encouragement they have made my life so much more worthwhile. Not only has my immediate family been awesome, but all my aunts, uncles, cousins, second cousins, extended family, etc. have also been really supportive.

Second, I have to say that my staff and customers at ReginaStyle have made this transition so much easier. When I came back home, they could easily have made me an outcast and judged me for my past transgressions. Instead they welcomed me with open arms and made me feel at home. Not many work environments would have made my coming home so enjoyable. The customers are just the greatest people ever. They never looked at me differently and were always kind and understanding. Even though I'm no longer at the shop, they continue to ask how I'm doing. I really miss the salon.

Third, are my amazing friends. Despite the fact that I was the one who changed, they went out of their way to do "sober fun" activities with me. Whether it was hiking, going to the gym, lunches, dinners, movies…the list could go on and on. It was really a huge sigh of relief when they still included me in all their activities and were constantly looking out for my best interest.

Last, but definitely not least, my church families at Hope Chapel Manaolana and Waialae Baptist Church. It must not have been easy to see someone born and raised in the church go so far down the road to destruction. I was initially hesitant to go back; however, those fears were completely unfounded. Christ-like love has always been shown by these church members, and their prayers are greatly appreciated.

In conclusion, I have been really blessed to be surrounded by so many people who have helped make my life what it is today. I only wish that others struggling with sobriety could be as fortunate as I am. I would like to ask all those who know someone battling addictions to help them as much as others have helped me. This is a battle that, without the help of others, would be impossible to win.

Don't judge; just love them. Don't think you can't make a difference; every prayer is heard. Don't ever give up; hope is often the last thing someone has. Don't make light of this disease; it's one that kills every day. You can make a difference in someone's life. You can be the light in a very dark world. Most importantly, someone, somewhere can use a helping hand. I did, and to those that reached out to help me…Thank You.

2 Corinthians 1:7   August 14th, 2008

"And our hope for you is firm, because we know that just as you share in our sufferings, so also you share in our comfort." 2 Corinthians 1:7

Sometimes I feel very alone here in California. I am accustomed to being able to go out anytime I want. Back home there was always someone I could call to grab a bite to eat, see a movie, or just plain hang out. I've learned that despite all my talk that God was my source of strength, I didn't rely on him 100% of the time. When times got rough, I sought out the company of others to console me.

This verse has taught me that in the end, God is the only One who can really understand my hurts, frustration, and pain. For the first time in a long time, I don't have that group of friends to rely on, and this has forced me to seek out comfort from Someone I cannot see or audibly hear.

When I'm at my lowest point, God provides in ways that show me just how awesome He really is—an unexpected phone call from a friend, text messaging that goes back and forth for hours, or emails that bring a smile to my face.

Even though things haven't been a piece of cake here in Cali, the thought of giving up has never crossed my mind. I have remained firm in my conviction that a personal relationship with Christ is the only way to success. Because of my faithfulness in Him, He has provided for all my needs and more.

Choices   August 15th, 2008

Obedience vs. Sin. Love vs. Hate. Peace vs. Anger. We all have choices to make in life. Many times the right thing to do is not necessarily the easiest thing to do. Every day I am faced with choices. Sometimes the answer is very clear; oftentimes it is clouded and difficult to see what the right course of action should be.

The only way I can be sure that what I'm doing is right is to maintain constant contact with God. Recently I've caught myself not being as diligent in my turning to Christ for answers. Instead I would call, text, or email someone from home and ask what I should do. While hearing the voice of loved ones is always nice, is that really where I need to be getting my answers?

What was striking was that it was someone who doesn't have a close relationship with God who asked me, "Have you prayed about it?" After that conversation, I made the choice to always ask for prayer when calling my Christian friends. Just because I've worked on my personal relationship with Christ doesn't mean that I won't make mistakes, but luckily the errors are not as severe as they once were.

The hard part is admitting when I make my mistakes. This week I got hired for the position I had really wanted; however, now I will be taking online courses instead of attending classes in Lakewood. Earlier I wrote about my decision to attend that particular school and have to admit that I was wrong. The choice I made at the time was not the correct one.

Looking back on the past couple of months, I find that mostly I've made the right choices. Even those that were wrong were not that big of a deal. It all stems from basing most of my decisions on the WWJD (What Would Jesus Do) mantra. It may be corny, but when I actually turn to the right source for my answers, it works.

Faithfulness   August 17th, 2008

"Do not cast away your confidence, for it carries a great reward." Hebrews 10:35

Today I got a call from the rehab center that I really, really wanted to work for. For the past few days I had started to wonder, "When am I going to get hired?" For a brief moment, I began to doubt if I was doing what God wanted me to do.

Looking back on how everything transpired, God was in control the whole time. I've been able to get settled in, met a couple of new friends, started a routine at the gym, meetings, Bible study, etc. However, I was beginning to get bored and needed to take things to the next level. Overall the timing couldn't have been better.

I know the boss, the manager, and at least half of the people I'll be working with. The facility is top-notch and has been featured on the show *Intervention*. Yes, I am really blessed to be in a position where I can learn from the best.

I don't know if it's a coincidence, but yesterday's entry ended with "because of my faithfulness in Him, He has provided all my needs and more." This job opportunity is totally because of my faith that God would provide.

Last year there was no way I would have taken this job. The pay is not what I'm used to. I'm starting at the bottom, and the job title is nothing to be super proud of. However, I will have the opportunity to share on a daily basis who my source of strength is. Most importantly, I will be able to offer hope to others that they can overcome their addictions.

Relationships   August 18th, 2008

Today in church the pastor talked about admitting your faults and realizing what you need to work on. My main weakness is relationships. I don't know if it all stems from my mother's illness or my grandfathers' passing away three months apart. Maybe after this entry, I'll have a better understanding.

Relationships have been really tricky for me. I've had plenty of practice so you would think I would be better at them. Sadly, that's not the case. I think seeing the relationship that my parents have has set the expectation bar very high. I see a couple that are best friends, and when they said, "'til death do us part," they meant every word.

I'm not saying that the bar is too high—it's just that I've not been willing to take the steps to allow someone to get that close to me. The fear of intimacy paralyzes me. People say that I just haven't met the right woman yet, and they're probably right. At the same time, I wouldn't know the right woman if she landed on my lap.

When someone gets close to my heart and I start to have genuine feelings, I start to think, "Will I stand by her if she gets sick? Would she stand by me if I get sick?" It's kind of unreasonable to put that on someone within such a short time of knowing her.

I also have this insane idea that if there's an argument within the first year, see ya later. I've seen so many marriages fail due to constant fighting, and I don't want to be a statistic. Having parents that seem to hardly ever fight reinforces my viewpoint. What I have come to learn over time is that my parents don't always agree on things; they just come to a compromise. The only way that happens is through time and working things out.

Another factor in my relationship issues is that when I lost my grandfathers, I felt totally helpless. It didn't matter how much I loved them; they still passed away. The hurt of losing them was unbearable. It's only been recently that I've been able to think of them and shed tears of joy. I bring that up because today in the service they sang this song (which I can't seem to remember at the moment), and I thought of my Grandpa Dominy. Tears came streaming down my face.

The song just made me remember all the great times I had with him. In a weird way I felt that he was there with me telling me, "I'm proud of you." Words cannot explain what he meant to me. He treated me like a son, and I would spend crazy amounts of time with him. He never missed a sporting event, piano recital, or choir performance. If my dad was there, I could count on my grandpa being there, too.

Shortly after I graduated from high school, my grandpa got sick and had to start kidney dialysis. It was hard for me to witness his decline. I would sleep in the hospital bed next to him while he had his transfusions. I drove him to the emergency room more times than I can count and sat with him in numerous doctors' offices. Memories of seeing him in pain are something I cannot let go of.

The sad part was that when he was in ICU and close to death, I disappeared. I flaked out and was nonexistent. The guilt that I carried for well over a decade crushed my spirit. Occasionally I still regret my actions during his last days alive. I vividly remember the day the family decided to pull the plug and let him go. If it weren't for a phone call from Val Kido (a church member) convincing me to visit, I would never have had a chance to say goodbye.

Driving to the hospital, I asked God to just let me hear, "I love you" one more time from Grandpa. I never heard those words. Instead it took at least five deacons from the church to remove me. I was inconsolable. My grandfather died an hour later. While I used that unanswered prayer to fuel my rage at God, I missed out on something amazing.

When I finally got sober, my mom reminded me of some things I seemed to have forgotten about that night. First, the nurses asked who I was for it was the moment that I left the ICU that his vitals had started to shut down. Grandpa had waited for me to come to say goodbye. Second, when I was in the room I saw a tear roll down his face when I said I loved him. People in comas don't cry. That was God's way of answering my prayer. Third, when the family went in to see him after he passed away, he had a smile on his face. He was finally at peace, and I like to think that that smile formed when he saw Jesus in heaven. As I sit here, tears are streaming down my face because even though I know he is in a better place, I still miss him.

I want to bring back the experience I had in church because not only did I feel that he's looking down from heaven saying he's proud of me, but it's also that he always loved me. Through all the crap that I went through, he was my guardian angel. I just closed my eyes, tears flowing, and saw him. Not as the sick dying man in ICU Room 13, 3rd floor at Saint Francis Hospital—the one with bloated feet from all the toxins, tubes sticking out—but the grandfather who loved me unconditionally, the one with a huge smile on his face.

Will this admission of what has hindered me in building solid relationships help? I honestly have no idea. What I do know is that writing this has reminded me of what love is about. It is unconditional.

Be Still   August 20th, 2008

"Be still, and know that I am God." Psalm 46:10

With the craziness that has been my life for the last month and half, this verse makes me remember that through it all, God is in control. I'm not used to living with others—constant noise and especially the crying of a two-year-old. Today I started working with addicts and alcoholics, and that is not a piece of cake.

It's in the quiet parts of the day (which are few) when I'm able to have peace. As my walk with God continues to grow, I'm able to have peace even when things are chaotic. No longer do circumstances dictate my state of mind. Rather it is how I respond to the situation. There is a "peace which surpasses all understanding" that can only be attained when I put my absolute faith in Christ.

In the past I would run from my problems and drown myself in a sea of drugs and alcohol. Now when things are difficult I try my best to turn things over to a power greater than myself.

When I fail, it can be pretty brutal. Even when I turn to Him, it doesn't mean that things are a bed of roses. The only constant is that when I give it to God, I stay sober.

<u>Day 2</u>   <u>August 21ˢᵗ, 2008</u>

Day 2 of working at the treatment center is complete. So far the job has been easier—both physically and mentally—than I had thought it would be. Emotionally, it is a million times harder. I'm working at the same facility that I went through to get sober, and I've been having flashbacks of the people who were there with me. The realization that the lives of other people are partially in my hands only heightens my emotional stress.

The staff remembers my group as one of the most eccentric and crazy collection of clients they had ever seen. The director even commented he didn't know how I got sober with all the distractions and setbacks that took place during my stay. It's rare that two people from the same group die within days of leaving the facility.

The memories of Tait are some of the hardest to handle. His death was part of the reason I dedicated my sobriety to helping others struggling with addiction. At times I look at the current group and see Tait in some of them. I pray that over time I will be able to let Christ-like love show and give these guys hope.

Even though I've only been around them for two days, I have a heart for each one of them. Deep down, I know that not all of them will be able to overcome the disease. It hurts knowing that a few of them won't make it to next year alive or without being jailed. The emotional rollercoaster is something I cannot bear on my own. It has forced me to further rely on God for my source of strength.

Each day is going to be a battle of good vs. evil. Satan already has a hold on those that I will be helping each day. It's only through prayer that a miracle will happen—the miracle of a new life. For those of you who read my blogs, I am humbly asking you to pray that God would give me wisdom to know what to say, discernment to know how to say it, and humility to know when to just shut up and pray.

Hope   August 22nd, 2008

I've been bringing up the term "hope" in a majority of my writings. The meaning of hope is "a feeling of expectation and desire for a certain thing to happen". When dealing with addictions, many times hope is elusive. I'm reminded of this while working at the rehab center. What's great is seeing hope return to someone who at one point didn't have any hope left.

When I finally hit rock bottom and was hopeless, that was when I began my recovery. I realized I couldn't continue living the life I was drowning in. Despite all the outside appearances of having fun, I was miserable. The nightlife scene had reduced me to a shell of the person I once was. The drugs and alcohol had taken a toll to the point that during the last five or six months of my addiction, I rarely left the house.

The night clubbing and bar life had lost its appeal. I didn't want to be around anyone because the additions had taken over. My main priority was staying high for as long as possible. In the end, I felt that without drugs and alcohol I could not live. What I've come to accept is that without Christ I cannot live.

The world is a cold and heartless place—full of lies, cheating, and stealing. It's no wonder I had no hope. I was stuck in a cycle that just plain hurt. The pain and anguish brought me to my knees. When I'd lost all hope of getting my life together, I asked for help. By the grace of God, I had a family that loved me enough to send me to the best facility they could afford.

Being in rehab did help me get sober. It taught me about my disease. It allowed me to discuss my feelings and emotions with professionals who knew what to say. I encountered other people struggling the same way I was, which made me feel not so alone. However, the one thing to which I held on tightly was my personal relationship with Christ. I knew that the only way to overcome was through Him.

"May the God of hope fill you with all joy and peace as you trust in him, so that you may overflow with hope by the power of the Holy Spirit." Romans 15:13

The power that Satan held over my life was a 13-year descent into my own personal hell. It was when I finally turned to God that joy and peace returned. As the scripture says, our God is one of hope. I had a desire and expectation to get clean and sober that was fulfilled by an awesome and loving God.

Time   August 23rd, 2008

When working in the recovery field, I guess becoming jaded is something that happens; it's sad but true. If I ever get that way, I'll find something else to do. The lives of others are in the hands of those who are helping them.

Today work was great. I was able to connect with all the guys that are going through the program. It's such a blessing to see these guys coming out of their cocoons and starting to see the light at the end of the tunnel. I won't kid myself and think that every single one will make it; the only thing I can do is try my best to offer them a glimmer of hope.

I try to make them feel that I'm one of them; in reality, I am one of them. I battle the same addictions they do. The only difference is that I have more sobriety time. At least that's what they think. I still hold on to what I was told. When I asked Ty, my first sponsor, how much time he had, he asked, "What time did you wake up today?" I said "7 a.m." He replied, "Well, you have five more hours than I do today because I didn't get up 'til 12."

Sobriety is a daily thing. The moment I let my guard down is the day I may relapse. I take it very seriously. I appreciate every moment that I'm not high or drunk. It's a gift that has many different aspects to it, but I never forget what makes up 99.9% of my success: Christ.

Giving Hope   August 25th, 2008

Two guys from the transition house (the next step after rehab) relapsed one day out of treatment. It was a stark reminder of how fragile sobriety can be. I think I'd forgotten how cunning and evil addictions are. It brought back memories of the group I went through rehab with.

Within the first month of getting out, I had to deal with two guys dying and over half of the group relapsing. Six months later, another 50%, and by the time I achieved one year, I was one of only two that had made it. Feelings of anger, disappointment, frustration, and fear flooded my soul. It was only by putting my faith in God that I was able to overcome them.

I had some one-on-one time with one of the guys who was struggling with the news that his friends had relapsed so soon. I was able to share my story and really empathize with what he was feeling. Seeing the lights go on and hope return brings a feeling I cannot explain. In a work environment where you see people struggling and failing on a daily basis, giving someone hope is simply amazing.

<u>Step 1</u>   <u>August 26th, 2008</u>

Step 1: We admitted we were powerless over alcohol, that our lives had become unmanageable. I am not a 12-Step fanatic, but I have come to appreciate this simple saying. Working with alcoholics and addicts has shown me how vital this step is. Until there is an acknowledgement of the sickness, no amount of treatment will help.

With the recent relapse of two clients, I noticed that they never took their disease seriously; they came in for a 28-day mini-vacation. It's sad to see that they had an opportunity to get sober but instead flushed it down the toilet. In retrospect, I could say the same thing for most of the guys in my group who have relapsed.

The key to admitting that you are powerless is finding where you are going to get your help. A doorknob, third moon goddess from Venus, or Jesus Christ; I think the answer is obvious. It's John 3:16 that gives me hope to defeat addictions: "For God so loved the world that He gave His only Son, that whoever BELIEVES in Him shall not perish but have eternal life."

God loves me so much that He was willing to send Jesus to die on the cross for all my sins. His sacrifice cleared the way that no matter how horrible and evil I once was, everything is forgiven. I understand that there are some chemical imbalances that affect sobriety. I also know that for me guilt played a role in my descent into an unmanageable cycle of addiction.

When I was able to grasp the concept of Christ's love, I realized that ALL my sins were forgiven and that rescue from my disease was only a prayer away. I'm not saying that once you pray, everything is going to be okay. It's a constant journey to have a better relationship with God. I have to be diligent in my pursuit of living a Christian life. That means reading the Word, praying daily, and abstaining from my sinful nature.

I've had people argue that if God loves them so much, why can't prayer be enough? Why do they have to work so hard to succeed? The best analogy I've heard is that God is like a personal trainer; He's there to get your life in shape. Unless you work out spiritually, you will never achieve your goals. You can go to the gym, but if all you do is stare at the weights, nothing will happen. If you put the time into following instruction and working out, amazing things can happen.

It's Totally Worth It   August 27th, 2008

"With this in mind, we constantly pray for you, that our God may count you worthy of his calling, and that by his power he may fulfill every good purpose of yours and every act prompted by your faith. We pray this so that the name of our Lord Jesus may be glorified in you, and you in him, according to the grace of our God and the Lord Jesus Christ." Thessalonians 1:11-12

My purpose in life is to help those struggling with addictions. These verses remind me that my life is supposed to bring glory to God, not myself. The 12-Step Program says that alcoholics are selfish, self-centered, and egotistical. I can be that way even when drugs and alcohol are not in the picture. As I continue on my journey, I need constant reminders to keep God first.

It is through Christ's strength that I am where I am today. My faith in Him allows me to proceed even when the going gets tough. This last week has been a real testament to how great God is. I've worked the last eight days straight with shifts going back and forth from 7:30 a.m. 'til 4 p.m. and 3:30 p.m. 'til midnight.

On my own, I would never have been able to recover from the hours. However, because I'm relying on God, I still look forward to going into work. Best of all, I've been able to maintain the mental, physical, emotional, and spiritual strength to minister to the clients.

I have to be at work in less than seven hours, and I'm happy. The reward of helping others far outweighs being tired and exhausted. As I sit here typing this entry, I can't wait to be back at the facility. I only wish that others could experience seeing people who are struggling take steps to living a better life. The joy that I feel every day is not muted by the reality of what may happen when they leave rehab. At the same time, I know that if they rely on God, anything is possible.

In a Little While   August 28th, 2008

In a Little While by Amy Grant

Days like these are just a test of our will.
Will we walk or will we fall?
Well, I can almost see the top of the hill,
and I believe it's worth it all.

In a little while we'll be with the Father; can't you see Him smile?
In a little while we'll be home forever. In a while....
We're just here to learn to love him;

we'll be home in just a little while.

When I was growing up, Amy Grant was my favorite artist. I recall putting in her tapes (yes, tapes; CDs were not yet invented) and sang along to all her songs. I guess I forgot about her during my years of self-destruction because if I had remembered this song, I think life would've been a whole lot easier.

The words have profound meaning if you really read between the lines. Life really is a hard road that has many pitfalls and heartache. She sings that even through the rough times, we get reminders of His love and that our purpose is to get to know Him more. If I can focus on the great gift that Jesus offers me through His death on the cross, the little bumps in the road are really nothing to worry about.

One day we will be reunited with an awesome Father who is waiting for us to turn to him. I can picture coming home to Hawaii while listening to this song—that my mission here in California is not a lifelong thing—that I'll be home... in a little while. Until then, I have Christ, and He will take care of all my needs.

I have a great family who loves and supports me. I have fantastic friends who check in on me from time to time. I'm living in a home that has people who care about me and make me feel part of their family. I work in a facility where I can be a servant to those who are fighting for their lives.

Through it all, God has been a faithful Father who I will see one day soon. When I do, I know He can say, "Job well done, my son. For all the years of rebellion and angst, you made a difference in the lives of others. Welcome home."

Forgiveness   August 29th, 2008

"Don't you see how wonderfully kind, tolerant, and patient God is with you? Does this mean nothing to you? Can't you see that his kindness is intended to turn you from your sin?" Romans 2:4

As someone who ran from God's love for 13 years, I often felt that I had sinned so horribly that there was no way God could forgive me. The guilt that I held onto was another excuse for me to go out and party. The shame and helplessness drove me deeper into depression and sin.

While talking to others struggling with addictions, I've found that a common theme is not being able to forgive ourselves for what we've done. Romans clearly lays out how awesome God's unconditional love is. He remains by our side even while we continue to sin. There are consequences for our actions yet we are reminded that He never leaves us. It is we who run from His tender mercy.

Another example that exemplifies God's forgiveness of all our sins is Jesus' death on the cross. He had two criminals next to him who were condemned to death. While one was unrepentant and mocked Christ, the other accepted that Jesus was Lord. Despite all the evil that he had done, Jesus told him that he would be in heaven with Him that day.

The hard part of dealing with addictions is that I used my self-loathing and low self-esteem to fuel my problems. I refused to fully accept that all my sins were forgiven because Satan had put blinders on me. As my drug and alcohol abuse grew, my personal relationship with Christ shrank.

Today it is by the grace of God that I have my life restored. The restoration of my life coincides with my walk with Him. The closer I get to God, the more I accept His love, the more I realize that He has forgiven my sins, and that allows me to forgive myself.

Power of Prayer   August 31st, 2008

The power of prayer is something I'm able to witness on a daily basis. First of all, there is the miracle of my sobriety. More than any meeting, group therapy, advice from my sponsor, etc., prayer is the one aspect of my life to which I attribute 99% of my success.

It's my personal time with God that allows me to seek direction in what I'm to do with my life. It's also in times of weakness and despair that I have Him to rely on. The one thing I've noticed is that I'm also praying more when my life is in order and going well. Thanking God daily for where I am reminds me that it's in the good times and the bad times that He is there.

I never forget that I'm fortunate enough to have people praying for me on a daily basis. My family, church family, and friends have been so awesome in praying for God to keep His hand upon me at all times. Recently I had the opportunity to have some prayer time with the guys I'm working with. Experiencing the presence of the Holy Spirit is something I cannot put into words.

There is one particular client with whom I've had an opportunity to share how God has worked in my life. He is a younger version of me—born and raised in the church and who happens to be trying to do things counter to what God has planned. While I cannot give clinical advice, what I can do with him is pray. It's a great experience seeing him want to have a better relationship with Christ.

I'm asking those of you who read my blogs to pray not only for me but also for those I'm working with. Many people don't have the prayer warriors that I have. I'm blessed to have hundreds of people praying for me, and I know that it's only through diligent prayer that I'm alive today. Prayer is a powerful tool that can be used to defeat the devil, and right now, the people I'm with are in the grips of Satan's evil grasp and need all the help they can get.

I'm Tired   September 1st, 2008

I don't usually write this late, and my brain feels like mush. I'm training for the graveyard shift and I'm super tired. Yesterday I could've been sleeping and getting ready for my shift, but a new client went on a little run and disappeared for an hour. Since I knew the guy really well, I decided to come down early and look for him. How did I know him so well if he was new? Because he had gone through the program with me last year.

In the past year, I've moved forward with my life and he seems to have digressed deeper and deeper into his addiction. We had the same case manager, same meetings, same classes, etc. How could two people who had the same training come out so vastly different? I honestly have no clue, but I have a hunch that my determination and walk with the Lord has played a huge role.

I was determined that I would overcome this disease. I took direction from others, listened to what my sponsor advised, and most importantly, turned everything over to God. What I'm seeing is that most of the people who have relapsed didn't want sobriety badly enough to totally turn over their will. I realize that my will got me into rehab; God's will saved my life.

From the Inside Out   September 4th, 2008

From The Inside Out by Hillsong United

A thousand times I've failed; still your mercy remains.
And should I stumble again, still I'm caught in your grace.
Everlasting, Your light will shine when all else fades.
Neverending, Your glory goes beyond all fame.
In my heart, in my soul, Lord I give you control.
Consume me from the inside out, Lord.
Let justice and praise become my embrace
To love You from the inside out.
Your will above all else, my purpose remains
The art of losing myself in bringing you praise.

I've had the opportunity to share with the guys about my personal relationship with Christ and how it has affected my life in sobriety. I've been asked to pray with at least six of the 14 men going through treatment. This song exemplifies that, even though I've failed—not a thousand times but probably a million times— when I give control to God, miracles can happen.

I don't deserve to be sober. In reality, I probably should not be alive today. It's only through God's mercy and grace that I still have a brain that works. While realizing how special my recovery has been, it's something that makes me remember my first night in rehab. I got on my knees and prayed that if I was going to struggle with addictions, I didn't want to wake up. However, if I did wake up, I would dedicate the rest of my life to helping those struggling with addictions.

Over the past 16 months I've embraced my faith and relied on God to guide me through rough times. My will got me into rehab; God's will saved my life. "Losing myself in bringing you praise" is a part of the song that many times I cannot sing. I get too emotional to finish that verse. I cannot give just a part of me to God; He wants all of me—mind, body, and spirit.

As long as I put God's will before my will, He will not only bless me but also those that I'm around. This isn't me being cocky; it's just that if I have His will as my priority, I'll be less likely to hurt those around me. I'll be putting others before my own selfish needs and hopefully others can see how God has made a difference in my life and will, in turn, put their trust in Him.

Today I was able to see the fruit of living my life for God. Two of the guys I've been praying with are getting baptized on Sunday. If there's any reward, seeing them accept or rededicate their lives to God is more rewarding than words can say. Another amazing experience that happened recently is that while praying with one of the clients, he gave me a hug, started crying, and wouldn't let go. I had prayed that God would wrap His arms around him and just show him unconditional love, and for a brief moment, my arms were "God's arms" hugging him.

The best part of praying with all these guys is the unmistakable presence of the Holy Spirit. Every time I've prayed, the anointing of the Holy Spirit is there, and it is simply awe-inspiring. I do not have any delusions that each one will be sober from this day forward. But in the time that we spend together in the presence of God, it is an opportunity for them to connect to the ultimate "higher power".

Words of Encouragement   September 5th, 2008

Lord, I'm amazed by You and how You love me. I'm so blessed to be in a situation to help others. Being transformed from the person who led people down the path to destruction to, only one year later, giving hope to those who have very little is only possible because of a God who loves me unconditionally.

There is nothing that I've done to earn a second chance to get my life back on track. No amount of money or fame could buy the priceless gift of forgiveness. The only way that I've moved forward in my life can be attributed to my digging deeper in my walk the Lord.

Along the way He has sent countless people to encourage me. They have given me books to read, CDs to listen to, DVDs to watch, and words of encouragement that I hold onto dearly. One of the workers back home sent me letters all the time and each one ended with, "Jesus Loves You." That simple reminder was a God send. Her little notes went a long way in reconnecting me to my faith.

I work in a field where I encounter men searching for answers. The roads they have taken have resulted in their being in a 28-day rehab facility. Aside from praying for them daily, I also try to do what Sharon did for me—offer them words of encouragement and always tell them, "Jesus Loves You."

. . .   *September 9th, 2008*

I'm really struggling here in California this week. Relax, it has nothing to do with my sobriety. It's just a combination of things—work, family back home, and people relapsing left and right. Satan is kicking the crap out of me. One or two of the issues would be manageable, but with everything coming at one time, I'm a bit overwhelmed.

For the last four days, I've written nothing on my website because I was angry and bitter. It was a swift kick in the butt to remind me that these entries have nothing to do with me. Rather it has to be inspired by what God has to say.

Please pray that I have the wisdom to handle everything that is coming my way. The emotional toll that I'm going through hurts more than anything in the last 16 months. I don't have a clue what to do concerning my work situation. My family is going through some tough times with my grandma in the hospital. People close to me who are relapsing and overdosing are breaking my heart.

They say to HALT when making important decisions—to never make them when you are hungry, angry, lonely, or tired. Right now I am hungry to have people around me who don't suck the life out of me; angry that I have a difficult person to work with as a shift leader; lonely in the sense that I have no family around; and tired of all the crap that has been going on.

If this was an MMA fight I'd be the guy on the ground who just got floored by a jab and uppercut, barely holding onto consciousness because the choke hold is cutting off all the blood to my brain. I wonder if I've bitten off more than I can chew, working with recovering drug addicts in a treatment center full of sick people while also taking classes and dealing with homesickness. Did I hear God's instruction correctly or did I rush into this on my own accord?

A Prayer Answered   September 9th, 2008

It is simply amazing how fast God answers when you turn to Him for direction. Since I'm working the graveyard shift, I'm able to read the responses from an email (a copy of the last blog) that I sent out. In the span of only an hour, my whole perspective on current events has changed. The overwhelming theme was to not give up, to stick it out, and to trust in God.

The first reply had a link on insight about business cycles. After every success there are dips. The trick is to fight through the rough parts; the bigger success is right around the corner. It also emphasized that I need to remember to continue to focus on what I'm great at. For me, that is praying for those around me. Satan doesn't want me to be here and the only way to overcome his obstacles is through prayer at all times. I will continue to do what is necessary for my job but will not let the insecurities and pettiness of a co-worker sidetrack me from the greatest tool in fighting addiction…the power of prayer.

The second reply came from someone in my martial arts group and men's Bible study. He was able to break it down step by step into escaping from a choke hold. For me, my choke hold has been my work situation. The first step is to relax. The worst thing I could do is to get overexcited. I was reminded of the need to re-think my approach to certain people. The second step is to protect myself from further damage. I need to be extra diligent in what I say and do. The third step is to find the key to release the lock, to move on it as if my life depended on it even if it means turning my life upside down. I've struggled with the inability to trust God 100% and trying to figure out ways that I can fix things. The reality of the situation is that I can't do anything. I just have to rely on God. The fourth and final word of wisdom was to be patient and persevere. I think that is what God is really trying to teach me…patience.

While the first and second replies gave me the wisdom that I was so desperately searching for, the third reply brought tears to my eyes. My spiritual batteries were completely drained and I needed to have a prayer for me. Instead of giving commentary on it, I've decided to just copy and paste what Tabol wrote…..

"I think we are all going through a trial season right now which is good because that means God is doing something big and using us. But it is hard at times. I'm struggling with a bunch of stuff, too. Knowing that I'm not the only one brings me comfort though. It's like the fire in me is fading a little bit every day, and I don't want it to go out completely, but I'm not doing anything to prevent it from happening either. I'm lazy, basically—lack of motivation. Just thought I'd share. I will continue to pray for you, brother. Love and miss you. Take care. –Tabz"

I was foolish in trying to be a superstar who prayed for others without asking others to pray for me. Less than two hours after I sent out the request for prayer, my spirit is refreshed, my purpose is firm, and most of all, I'm reminded that I'm here for a reason… to share my story of how God changed my life, the amazing power of His love, and that it's in Christ alone that I put my trust.

More Answered Prayers   September 10th, 2008

The response to my request for prayer was a quick reminder of how loving God is. My mind was full of doubts, fear, and a lot of anger. Over the last 24 hours, I've been blessed to receive emails and phone calls from loved ones and the common theme was, "Don't give up." I usually write what I think God wants me to share; however, today's entry is dedicated to those who were His messengers.

It's been a real eye opener to see how many people are praying for me back home. I guess I needed a reminder of how fortunate I am. Below are some of the emails I received and the words of wisdom that have changed my attitude in a way that can only be described as a miracle.

"God never promised the path through life to be easy. At times I've gotten so depressed that I felt that the struggle wasn't worth it. The only comfort I can often muster is my faith that God will never abandon us. As you may remember, I had many such moments while at Pac Hills. You, more than anyone, were an enormous help in getting me through those tough times. Our prayer sessions you led will be embedded in my memory forever. You helped me in ways that even I didn't understand at the time. I will never forget those moments. My trying to give you any solace in your struggles is like Tiny Tim giving instructions to the Rock before a wrestling match. But you must understand and believe that the prayers and comfort you have willingly and lovingly given me and countless others have been, and will continue to be, a source of peace that is needed in these trying times. I have no doubt in my mind that you can and will overcome the demons attacking you right now because you realize that God is now and always the source of our strength. Let Him carry these burdens for you, and I'm certain that tomorrow will be a better day. In my own little feeble way, I will pray for that to happen. —Alex"

"You are in my prayers BIG TIME! You are being obedient to God's calling on your life and trying to be obedient to His whispers. That gets the enemy angry! He will use whatever, whomever against you whenever he can. He'll attack the things that you value most, pick on the weakest and/or dearest, and mess with your head so that your priorities are out of order. But know that God is doing a good work in and through you. So cover yourself continually in Jesus' blood, knowing that His mercies are new every moment. Don't let the lies of the enemy distract or discourage you. Keep your eyes on Jesus so you can stay above the stormy seas. At mini-church last night, we were taking prayer requests. So many of us are in a funk, feeling detached from God. His voice is not loud and clear, but rather distant sometimes, even seemingly nonexistent. We decided to all read the same book in the Bible and come back and share next week. We also agreed that the Lord must be preparing us for something good, something big, and that we need to step it up in our personal relationship with Him and with each other. The enemy is the master deceiver, and he has us all wondering where God is and why He's so far away from us when in reality, He lives IN us! And His desire is for us to desire Him! Be encouraged and keep the faith! –Kathy"

"Reminds me to step up my prayers for you, bro. I'm not sure what to say to you except I think you know deep down where to go and what to recall. The Serenity Prayer comes to mind. I do feel for you with your heart for your family and what is happening right now. If there is something I can do to help, let me know. You're doing awesome work, Jon. Though the initial outcomes (relapses) do not reflect that, the real work is walking in obedience with God, putting up with some fools at work, and contending for them. I'm not as much worried about you inasmuch as I see a breakthrough coming soon. –John"

"Don't let failures around you define you. A great batting average is .300. Losing 70% of the time at bat would put you at the top of the league. I imagine trying to control someone else's addiction (which they probably took several years to develop) is a little more difficult than hitting a ball with a stick. I imagine it's a little bit like being a Little League coach and getting upset because each of the players didn't hit a home run on every at bat. Cut yourself some slack and make sure you are constantly feeding your mind and spirit with 'good food.' Then just let God do the rest. –Albert"

The Right Source   September 11th, 2008

With recent events, my perspective on what I'm doing here has taken on a whole new slant. All along I was under the impression that I was here to help others; in reality, my growth as a person was something I was overlooking. I cannot do this on my own. For a while I was relying on Jon to get things done; that was foolish, a mistake I'll try never to make again.

While writing these entries has been very therapeutic, I think I was getting a little big-headed. I was only giving advice on how to overcome addictions—*my* outlook, *my* stories, *my* insight, etc. I had lost focus on what the Bible has to say. A lot of what I've written is "fluff"—not much "meat." Utilizing my life stories and lyrics from songs is great, but that's not what sanitizeyoursoul.org is about.

In my Mission Statement, the first thing I write about is Biblically-based principles. I seemed to have strayed from that basic premise. I think the scripture below is an accurate verse that can explain the kick-in-the-butt that I got over the last week.

"When pride comes, then comes disgrace, but with humility comes wisdom. The integrity of the upright guides them, but the unfaithful are destroyed by their duplicity." Proverbs 11:2-3

I ask that you continue to pray for me, the people I work with, and the clients that I spend time with daily. I know God has me here for a reason—to share my story, yes, but also to use the Word of God as the foundation because on my own I am nothing.

Titus 3:3-6   September 12th, 2008

"At one time we too were foolish, disobedient, deceived and enslaved by all kinds of passions and pleasures. We lived in malice and envy, being hated and hating one another. But when the kindness and love of God our Savior appeared, he saved us, not because of righteous things we had done, but because of his mercy. He saved us through the washing of rebirth and renewal by the Holy Spirit." Titus 3:3-6

Wow! If there ever were verses that could accurately explain what drug and alcohol addiction is about, this is as close as it gets. I was foolish in walking down the easy path—disobedient in ways that still make my stomach turn, totally deceived by Satan's lies that my sins could not be forgiven, and sadly enslaved to a hedonistic lifestyle that eventually took me to rehab. I only wish that the people I work with could really grasp the power of what this scripture says.

Not only was my life filled with sin, malice, and envy; it was full of hate. Not only did I hate others, but hating who I was made things even worse. Even though I knew what I was doing was wrong, I still did it. In turn, I had this self-hatred that only fueled Satan's lies. Satan is one tricky character, and unless I have the power of Christ behind me, I'm in a battle I can never win. However, through Jesus' death on my cross, all those sins are forgiven regardless of what the devil wants me to believe.

There is nothing that I've said or done that has brought me the miracle of sobriety. It is His tender mercy and love that allows me to live life how it should be. The simple task of rededicating my life to Christ was the catalyst to overcoming Satan's evil stronghold on my life. When I asked the Holy Spirit to reign within me, I was reminded that I have the power to overcome everything Satan throws at me.

I am not perfect. My attitude this past weekend was horrible and probably very unpleasing to God. It shows that I'm still human. When I turned to God for help, His amazing mercy was once again evident. All the crap I was dealing with at work has been resolved, my loneliness has subsided, and my fear of my grandmother's condition is fading.

My walk with the Lord is a continual journey which will never be spotless. The expectation of perfection was another trap that Satan had set and I had fallen for. I was blinded and went into a funk that previously would have triggered an episode of drugs and alcohol. This time I turned to my loving Heavenly Father for help and, in turn, He gave me the reassurance and support of my wonderful family and friends.

P.S. To all who sent me emails, text messages, phone calls, and prayers, thank you very much.

Forgiving Others   September 15th, 2008

I have an anger problem. If someone does me wrong, I usually try to think of ways to make his life a living hell. My resentment and anger eventually led me down a dark road. Because I was unable to forgive others, I eventually came to believe that God could not forgive me of my sins.

The area of forgiving others is still a part of my life that I need to work on. While it is getting better, I still have to vent and go off on a mini-tangent before I'm reminded that, in the big scheme of things, I'm lucky to have been forgiven of my past transgressions.

"Bear with each other and forgive whatever grievances you may have against one another. Forgive as the Lord forgave you." Colossians 3:13

Today I was ticked off at someone; I had every right to be. His selfishness and ungratefulness got me to the point that I could care less what happens to him. The only time I get a phone call from this particular person is when he needs a ride. It's gotten so predictable that I don't even know why I pick up the phone. All I hear is "I need [this]," or "Why can't you do [that]?" Dealing with addicts is not an easy thing. In fact I have no reason to deal with his crap except that God dealt with my crap for many years.

If I'm really to say that my source of strength comes from God—that it is only through His mercy that I'm alive today—then maybe I need to re-examine my attitude. This doesn't mean that I'm going to become a doormat and become this guy's taxi driver. All it means is that I'm going to try and not let anger reside in my soul. Instead I need to forgive him of his blatant self-centeredness and simply love him as Christ loves me.

The fact of the matter is that I anger, irritate, and annoy others. I can be selfish, self-centered, and egotistical. Realizing my imperfections makes it easier to accept the crap that others throw my way. However, as the verse so clearly reminds me, I need to forgive as the Lord has forgiven me.

Wisdom   September 16th, 2008

"If any of you lacks wisdom, he should ask God, who gives generously to all without finding fault, and it will be given to him. But when he asks, he must believe and not doubt because he who doubts is like a wave of the sea, blown and tossed in the wind. That man should not think he will receive anything from the Lord; he is a double-minded man, unstable in all he does." James 1:5-8

I had always wondered why I couldn't have overcome addictions sooner. I had prayed that I didn't want to do drugs anymore and it just seemed that it was an unanswered prayer. While I am no Bible scholar, this verse spoke to me about why I continued on the road to self-destruction.

To start, most of my prayers came when I was unstable, still high or drunk. My prayers were not about staying sober; they were about taking away the crappy feeling of coming off of drugs. When

87

I realized that I would feel that way, I decided to never have the down; I'd just be high all the time. Talk about being stupid.

I can remember being so frustrated that I couldn't go to sleep. I prayed that if I was able to sleep, I would quit. I also recall being scared when my heart was beating a thousand times a minute. I prayed that if my heart rate would go down, I would get sober. The most ridiculous memory I have was of hallucinating and seeing demons battling angels. I prayed to make those thoughts go away. The bottom line is that I was not putting my trust in God; I was trying to make deals with Him.

The prayer that was answered was the one I prayed when I put my absolute faith in God. The wisdom I'd sought was given and hope was finally restored. I was at the weakest and most vulnerable point in my entire life. I knew that I could no longer live life my way; it was time to do things God's way. When I was able to humble myself before my Creator and truly turn to Him for help, He did it without question, without judgment, and in the end, with the blessing of sobriety.

Joy of the Lord   September 17th, 2008

"The LORD has done great things for us, and we are filled with joy."
Psalm 123:6

I don't think I've shared about how joyful my life is since I returned to God's loving arms. Recently I've been sharing quite a bit on the difficulties that I've been going through and the heartache of living a sinful life. The flip side to all the pain I endured for 13 years is the remarkable life that I'm blessed to have today.

In the past I could never stay at home. I was searching for something, someone, or someplace to go. It was a fruitless attempt to fill a void in my life that could never be filled. The girls, drugs, events, and nightclubs were an empty pleasure that never satisfied.

While the life I used to live had peaks and valleys, what I was lacking was joy. I'm now able to enjoy the simple things in life, like a nice sunrise while driving home from work after the graveyard shift, being healthy enough to work out at the gym and not feel that I will pass out from exhaustion, watching the Dallas Cowboys come back from the brink of defeat to storm back to a wonderful victory over the Philadelphia Eagles.

I've been fortunate to find activities that are fun, wholesome, and that bring me joy. Before I moved to the California, I really enjoyed my martial arts training group. My new found passion is going to 24-Hour Fitness, working out for about an hour, then relaxing in the sauna and Jacuzzi. While some people think that I need a different hobby and need to get out more, my answer is, "I was out and running amok for 13 years. I enjoy the peace and solitude I have today."

Whether it's overcoming drug addiction, alcoholism, anger issues, etc., what I have found is that when you are at peace with who you are and are following the path that God has laid out, joy can come in many shapes and sizes. Most nights that I write these entries I'm sitting in a garage listening to the insects make whatever noises they make and enjoying the cool breeze.

The Lord has provided me an opportunity that 17 months ago I would not have thought was possible. Not only am I sober, but I'm living a joyful life. Regardless of the obstacles that come my way, God's love allows me to overcome everything. Joy is such a powerful weapon against Satan, and he will try everything in his power to take it away. He knows that now "the joy of the Lord is my strength."

A Life Changed   September 18th, 2008

"And Jesus came and spoke to them, saying, 'All authority has been given to Me in heaven and on earth. Go therefore and make disciples of all the nations, baptizing them in the name of the Father and of the Son and of the Holy Spirit, teaching them to observe all things that I have commanded you; and lo, I am with you always, even to the end of the age. Amen.'" Matthew 28:18-20

I've been working at the treatment center for about a month. Tomorrow will be the first time a client will leave that I was able to spend the entire 28 days with. While it's selfish of me to say this, I don't want him to leave. I'm not allowed to play favorites, but since he is the first "full-term" person, he has a soft spot in my heart.

The transformation that I've seen in this young man is nothing short of amazing. Not only have I had the opportunity to pray with him but I was shocked when I heard him say that I've inspired him. When I heard this I almost cried.

It's been so long since I've been a positive influence on anyone. For years I was the one probably turning people away from Christ. They probably said, "Look at that hypocrite." Today is obviously a different story. While I prepared to write this blog tonight, a song came to mind: *Thank You* by Ray Boltz. The chorus is something I never thought would be possible with me.

Thank you for giving to the Lord.
I am a life that was changed.
Thank you for giving to the Lord.
I am so glad you gave.

While this job may not be financially rewarding, the hope that I'm able to give to others is simply amazing. One guy even asked me if I ever thought of becoming a pastor. While the question was flattering, to say the least, that is not my call in life. My call is to be in a field where the success rate is very low; however, I firmly believe that with Christ as the source of strength, miraculous things can happen.

Please be in continual prayer for all the men I minister to. For some, this is their last chance at life. One of the guys even told me that his original plan was to do the program and then go and commit suicide on the railroad tracks. I'd like to think that the reason he didn't follow through was because of the prayers from all of you. That same young man had a spiritual moment with God the other night. He got on his knees and asked God for help.

I led this entry with The Great Commission. It doesn't matter if you're working in a rehab facility, if you're a clerk at the grocery store, or the CEO of a large corporation, share who God is, live a life that is glorifying to Him, and love others like God loves you. Lives can be changed and souls can be saved.

My Shepherd   September 19th, 2008

"The LORD is my shepherd, I shall not be in want. He makes me lie down in green pastures, He leads me beside quiet waters, He restores my soul. He guides me in paths of righteousness for his name's sake. Even though I walk through the valley of the shadow of death, I will fear no evil, for you are with me; your rod and your staff, they comfort me." Psalm 23:1-4

I remember that when I was in sixth grade I had to memorize this verse. It's one of those that I can recite any time of day, but it wasn't until recently that I understood its significance.

My roommate from Pac Hills, whom I just happened to sponsor, is going to another treatment facility. He's battling heroin addiction and has blamed me for his recent relapse. He has accused me of not being there for him or that I can't be his "taxi driver" and pick him up whenever he's in need. While it's a silly excuse, it dawned on me that the Lord needs to be his Shepherd…not me.

When you have the Almighty God leading you to green pastures and quiet waters, no human can duplicate what He can do. The stress of everyday life is not so bad. It's because of His love that my spirit is restored. My life is no longer based on the circumstances around me; my life is guided by God's infinite wisdom.

The field I'm in is one where I'll be walking through the valley of the shadow of death. I'm not afraid of what Satan has up his sleeve. I'm very aware that he'll continue to attack me and make things as difficult as possible. What keeps me on track and focused on the job at hand is that I know that God is on my side fighting the battle for me.

I need to get out of the way, not try to do things on my own, and rely on Christ as my source of strength. My Shepherd, who is going to get me through the upcoming challenges, is a loving and caring God who also is one tough cookie. My God is not one to leave me to fend for myself. My God has already won every battle that is to come my way. All I have to do is follow him.

Comfort   *September 22nd, 2008*

"Praise be to the God and Father of our Lord Jesus Christ, the Father of compassion and the God of all comfort, who comforts us in all our troubles, so that we can comfort those in any trouble with the comfort we ourselves have received from God. For just as the sufferings of Christ flow over into our lives, so also through Christ our comfort overflows." 2 Corinthians 1:3-5

The 12th Step is having a spiritual awakening as the result of the previous steps. We try to carry this message to alcoholics and to practice these principles in all that we do. For me, 2 Corinthians gives the answer to helping others. It is to share the comfort that I've received with fellow alcoholics and addicts.

While I've completed "the steps" and see the validity of them, my belief is that it's my personal relationship with Christ that keeps me sober. I've recently begun sponsoring more guys, and I have this saying: "The steps helped me get sober, but my walk with the Lord is what keeps me sober."

The more I work with alcoholics and addicts, the greater is my resolve that God is the source of my strength. There is nothing I can do or say that will give the kind of comfort and grace that Christ can. All I can do is be a conduit—just share my story and pray with them.

I can give hope by living a joyful life and showing these men that it is possible; however, living separate from God, it is impossible. I can pray and offer guidance, but it's God who answers prayers. I'm a mortal human who, without the love and comfort of God, is unable to do much. However, when I let Christ's love overflow in all that I do, miracles can and will happen.

Working the Graveyard   September 23rd, 2008

I've been complaining recently about working the graveyard shift. It screws up my sleep schedule, I can't go to the gym as often as I'd like, and I feel like crap for a few days. In my eyes there's nothing of value working this shift. However, tonight I was able to pray and lead someone to the Lord.

Just last week one of the guys with whom I'd connected moved on to the transition house. While I was able to see him baptized on Sunday, I was kind of bummed that I wouldn't be seeing him as often. The connection we had was really awesome. I always looked forward to seeing him and sharing how God has changed my life.

I don't think it's a coincidence that the person who is now in his room is the guy that I was able to share with tonight. While A.M. (I have to use initials for confidentiality) was born and raised in the church like I was, the new guy D.B. has a parent who is really sick and a grandparent who is in poor health. After talking for a little bit and hearing what he was going through, I let him read my entry about my grandfather.

After he finished, we proceeded to talk a little more. Eventually, I asked if I could pray for him. When we were done, he had tears streaming down his face. He realized that he can't do this on his own and asked if I could help him get a Bible. I find it simply amazing that God can use me, a former drug-addicted drunk, to bring people to the Lord.

As you read this entry, I'm asking you to pray for all the guys that are in the facility. Pray that if they are searching for truth, peace, or are looking for their "higher power", that they will know they can have Christ as their source of strength. I've been here for a little over a month, and during that time K.T., A.M., M.B., and D.B. have accepted Christ or rededicated their lives. Please pray that as they battle addictions they will have a peace that passes all understanding, that they can one day be a light for others, and most importantly, that they stay sober.

My Week   September 24th, 2008

Recently I've had a few guys leaving the facility and they asked me what I do to stay sober. My answer is always the same: I put the same amount of effort into staying sober as I used to put into partying. Since I went to a bar or nightclub daily, I go to the gym daily. I did drugs a few times a day, so I read the Bible a few times a day.

Living a life of sin was really enjoyable for the first couple of years; however, in the end, it was full of disappointments and regrets. Today I choose to live a life that has very few regrets and even fewer disappointments. Since I'm still relatively new to this sobriety thing, I need to have structure in what I do. The repetitiveness makes walking the straight and narrow much easier.

Here's a look at my weekly schedule:
Sunday: Church in the morning, watching sports in the afternoon, and 24-Hour Fitness at night;
Monday: 24-Hour Fitness in the afternoon, work the graveyard shift;
Tuesday: Sleep 'til 1 p.m., 24-Hour Fitness at 2 p.m. and at 9 p.m.;
Wednesday-Saturday: 24-Hour Fitness in the morning, work from 3:30 p.m. 'til midnight.

I've become a creature of habit. The simplicity of following this schedule allows me security in knowing what comes next. Most times I don't even know what day it is but I can tell you what I will be doing all the time. The Bible talks about idle time as when Satan is at play. I cannot and will not allow the devil to have control of any part of my life. Even though each day is full of activities, I set aside time to pray and meditate on what the Word says.

Without the boundaries that I've set, I would be directionless. Without the regimen that I've set, I would have idle time. Each and every day, I devote the time and energy needed to remain sober. Not only has God blessed me with a new lease on life; He also had granted me peace and joy.

Saving Lives   September 25th, 2008

"Rescue those being led away to death; hold back those staggering toward slaughter." Proverbs 24:11

I've come to realize that this is exactly what I'm doing at my job. It's sad to see so many people struggling with addiction. It's a great reminder to me of how far I've come over the last 17 months. The disease of drug addiction and alcoholism is a killer; for some, this may be their last chance at life.

I can't imagine going through this kind of pain and anguish without having Christ as the power source. I was given an assignment today from the program director. I was asked to come up with scriptures for all 12 Steps. While researching I came across...

"But the Lord stood at my side and gave me strength, so that through me the message might be fully proclaimed and all the Gentiles might hear it. And I was delivered from the lion's mouth. The Lord will rescue me from every evil attack and will bring me safely to his heavenly kingdom. To him be glory for ever and ever." 2 Timothy 4:17-18

When I read this verse, it spoke volumes of how amazing my transformation has been. Without the Lord's saving me from myself, I would still be losing the battle. However, because He is so mighty and powerful, I really have nothing to fear.

If you had asked me 18 months ago what I'd be doing today, I would have said that I had no clue—probably drinking and drugging. For so long that was all I knew. By the grace of God, I am now making a difference in sick people's lives. I'm offering Hope to those with no hope, I'm sharing the Word of God with people searching for a god, and most importantly, I'm now leading people to Christ.

When people have everything in order, God is not too appealing. However, when they are broken and searching for answers, God is really the only answer. I sometimes wonder why it wasn't until I'd hit rock bottom that I turned to God. I think I just knew that He was the only one who could save me.

Still a Sinner   September 29th, 2008

I'm going home for a week in November. I can't put into words the joy that I'm feeling right now. While it will only have been five months since I left Hawaii, I miss a lot of things—my family, friends, people at Regina's, food, and of course, my doggies. While there are five dogs where I live, no animals can replace my Kapua and Happy.

I've learned so much since I moved. Probably more soul searching has been done than in all my previous 31 years. While I am sober, I've concluded that I'm still deficient in many areas— anger management, selfishness, women, ego, the list could go on and on.

While working at the treatment center I've had many guys come up and say that I've been a light for them. It's flattering, to say the least, yet God humbles me with this verse…

"For ALL have sinned and fall short of the glory of God."
Romans 3:23

Recently my ego has been a source of weakness. There are a few cocky clients that have really gotten on my nerves. I had to be reminded by my sponsor that I'm dealing with sick individuals. Even if they really tick me off, I need to give to them the same level of service as I give to people I get along with. It's a tough pill to swallow.

Through reading scripture I'm convicted to show Christ-like love to idiots. It's a daily struggle to put up with irritating, self-centered drunks and addicts except when I remember that, at one point, I was the irritating, self-centered drunk and addict. If God showed me love and placed people in my life to show me love, the least I can do is return the favor.

Doing the wrong thing is easy to do; doing the right and godly thing is nearly impossible to do on my own. However, because the Holy Spirit lives in me, "I can do all things through Christ who strengthens me." Philippians 4:19

Waiting on the Lord   September 30th, 2008

"But seek first his kingdom and his righteousness, and all these things will be given to you as well. Therefore do not worry about tomorrow, for tomorrow will worry about itself. Each day has enough trouble of its own." Matthew 6:33-34

It's sometimes very difficult for me to fully grasp this verse. Not worry about tomorrow? I usually worry what's going to happen a year from now. Putting my trust in God for my sobriety is easy because when it comes to dealing with drugs and alcohol, I've proved that I'm an idiot. When it comes to waiting for other things, that's a different story.

Right now I see a lot of people around me finding significant others. The guys leaving treatment have girlfriends and the ones who don't seem to find someone as soon as they get out in the "real world". Even my roommate has found someone. I sometimes think, "What is wrong with me? Why can't I find someone?"

I've had a horrible track record when it comes to finding the girl of my dreams. My dating history could be a movie…a horror movie. Since I've been sober, every time I thought I'd found "the one", I've prayed a simple prayer: "Lord, if she's the one, let me know and if not, then give me a clear sign that she's not the one." God has answered that prayer quicker than anything I've prayed for. Needless to say, I'm still single.

God has a funny way of reminding me of some of the things I've prayed about in the past. A few months ago I went on a 40-day, no-TV and no-meat fast. Before I started the fast, I wrote a list of things I'd be praying about. One of them was that I would no longer chase after women. If she's the one, God will just drop her in my lap.

There's a part of me that wonders, "Alright, God, I've been faithful and I'm waiting on You to show me who I'm supposed to be with so hurry up." Sometimes I can be a major pain in the butt. The only thing I know is that if I'm constantly dwelling on when He will show me who she is then that's less time I have to spend on my personal relationship with Christ.

Maybe God is teaching me patience. Maybe I'm just not ready to be in a relationship. I've decided that instead of worrying about why God is making me wait, I'm just going to continue to put my trust in Him and live today to the best of my abilities.

Perspective   October 1st, 2008

Today was a blah day. I worked the graveyard shift and didn't get home till 8:15-ish, slept 'til 2-ish, went to the gym twice, and am finally writing this entry. This was a million times more productive than what my life was for 13 years. One of the things I've learned over the last year is perspective.

According to the dictionary, *perspective* is defined as "a particular attitude toward or way of regarding something; a point of view". I can choose to focus on the positive or dwell on the negative. When I was abusing drugs and alcohol, I chose to think about what was wrong with my life, and it drove me to use even more. While life is still full of obstacles, I've decided that I'll find what is positive and move on from there.

"Finally, brothers, whatever is true, whatever is noble, whatever is right, whatever is pure, whatever is lovely, whatever is admirable—if anything is excellent or praiseworthy—think about such things." Philippians 4:8

If I choose to be negative and pick apart every single detail of what upsets me, I'd probably be back using drugs and drinking. What this verse says is that I would be wasting my time. Even in the darkest of moments there is a silver lining...I just have to find it.

A clear example was a phone call I had last night. One of the guys who had left the facility called and informed me that a bunch of ex-clients had relapsed. My spirit was down; I felt defeated. All the talks and encouragement I had given were now meaningless.

Through the course of our discussion, I kept reminding him that it doesn't matter what others are doing; what matters is whether he himself is sober. Whenever he was feeling down about the situation, I would ask, "Are you sober?" and each time I would say, "Just focus on that." In a roundabout way, I was also giving myself a pep talk. Even though five of them reverted to drugs, one of them is still sober.

I'm sad to hear that in less than a month after leaving a $20,000 stay in rehab, five guys are back to using and abusing. At the same time, I'm grateful that the one I've been sharing scripture with is still sober. With the vision that God has placed on my heart, perspective is going to play a part in how I view the quality of work that I do.

Good vs. Evil   October 2nd, 2008

"Test everything. Hold on to the good. Avoid every kind of evil." 1 *Thessalonians 5:21-22*

Good vs. Evil. It doesn't get any simpler than that. Every single choice in my life boils down to the basic premise of good and evil. As simplistic as it is, it doesn't make life any easier. Many times what feels right and brings immediate gratification is not necessarily what is in my best interest in the long run.

I used to complicate and make excuses for my actions. I would not feel that I needed to be held responsible for what I did.

Eventually that train of thought led me down the path to hell. No matter what lies Satan tells me, there's always a right and a wrong way of doing things. The main difference in how I live today is that I read what the Word of God says which means all my answers can be found in the Bible.

I notice that the more I read and study scripture, the decisions I have to make get a lot clearer. It doesn't mean that making those choices gets any easier, just a lot clearer. If I was to revert to my old way of doing things and not have a conscience, I would be in trouble.

While writing these entries is meant to help others get and stay sober, I've found that it has made my personal relationship with Christ even stronger. I've never shared how I choose which verses to write, and it's a lot simpler than some may think. Depending on my current emotion, feeling, or event, I punch a word in the concordance and voilà...out pops a couple of verses. Sometimes I read 10 verses before something speaks to me; other times it's the first verse that comes up.

Over the last three months of writing, I've been blessed to read more about what the Bible has to say than I've read in the last 13 years combined. I don't think that it's a coincidence that over the same period of time I've been able to differentiate between good and evil much better than I ever have in the past. In the process, I've chosen to hold onto the Word of God and avoid the lies that the world has told me.

Need vs. Want   October 6th, 2008

"I tell you the truth, anyone who has faith in me will do what I have been doing. He will do even greater things than these, because I am going to the Father. And I will do whatever you ask in my name, so that the Son may bring

glory to the Father. You may ask me for anything in my name, and I will do it." John 14:12-14

There is a self-centered part of me that, when I read this verse, thought about a lot of materialistic things. The list I had in mind would take up pages upon pages of selfish wants. What I appreciate is that while I still don't have that brand new house on Hawaii Loa Ridge, God has provided for all my needs.

Recently I've experienced what struggling financially means. I've never had this horrible thing called rent. I was blessed to always have a refrigerator filled with wonderful food. If I ever needed something and didn't have the funds at the time, there was always Dad to ask. Now I have rent to pay, there are groceries to buy, and I don't have the luxury of having Dad to ask for help. However, the Lord has provided everything I need. The most amazing thing is that despite the added bills, I actually have a savings/checking account that isn't empty or overdrawn.

Over the last few months I've really begun to understand how fortunate I've been my whole life. It's forced me to grow up and take more responsibility that I ever had in the past. While I'm not living the life of a king, I'm content with what I have. I'm able to go to one of the best 24-Hour Fitness gyms in California, I still have my HDTV and am able to watch all my football games, and most importantly, I still have my sobriety.

All the needs I've prayed for have been supplied. Some things have even been given to me! I continue to be amazed at how the Lord provides. Every once in a while I'll get a check in the mail from an unexpected source, and usually it's when I had started to stress about not having enough money.

It's nice to know that I've been provided a support network back home that not only prays for me but sends snacks, DVDs, letters of encouragement, and other things. God has provided everything I need and then some. He's made the transition to California as easy as I ever could have dreamed possible.

Mind of the Spirit   October 7th, 2008

"The mind of sinful man is death, but the mind controlled by the Spirit is life and peace." Romans 8:6

For people struggling with drug addiction and alcohol, the first part of this verse is dead on...eventually it will lead to death. But when we turn to Christ, He grants us life and a peace that passes all understanding. I can remember one of the times that I went to the emergency room and the nurse told me she didn't know how I was still alive. While working at the rehab center, I've found that I'm not alone. Many of those battling addiction share my story.

The sad part is that not everyone is as fortunate as I've been. Within two months of getting out of treatment, one of the guys I went to the program with overdosed and died. I've also had my ex-roommate to OD a few times; once he had to be brought back to life. The main difference between myself and the others? I have the Holy Spirit residing in me. It's through divine intervention that I've been able to overcome my demons and find peace.

Without peace from the Lord, I have no clue how I could still be sober. The heartache and pain that I once had would've overwhelmed me. It's only by casting all of my cares on Christ that I can deal with the disease of drug addiction. Sometimes I wish there was a way I could brainwash those who try to do this without God and re-program their minds to trust in the Lord. The more I think about that, the more I understand that if that's how God wanted it, He would have programmed humans to obey Him. The fact of the matter is that we have a choice—a choice to do right or to do wrong, a choice to have a mind like Christ or to have a mind of sin.

Just One   October 8th, 2008

Just one. While watching a program on ESPN about how they use basketball to help drug addicts, this was the phrase used by the head of the program to explain his attitude. Sometimes I get down when I see so many people failing at sobriety. Despite all the effort I put into my job, the success rate isn't that high.

There are many factors when it comes to people relapsing. Right now I just don't feel like listing the many reasons that lead someone to going back down the path to a life of hell. In my opinion, a lack of personal relationship with Christ is a major factor. It can be easy to be depressed about the situation, but when I heard the phrase, "just one", a light came on.

I still believe that statistics can be changed and that one day I'll be able to influence more people into living a joyful life in sobriety. But until that day comes I consider myself blessed that even though I may be the one that stays sober, that is what I need to accept.

It would be nice to see tangible results every single day; however, I need to see the bigger picture. The seeds that I'm planting may not come to fruition immediately but somewhere down the road that seed may grow into a large oak tree that will affect the lives of more people than I ever could. Who knows, maybe someone that I'm sharing with will go on to become a "Billy Graham" for addicts. The fact of the matter is that before I can reach thousands, I need to start with "just one".

Amazing   October 9th, 2008

A day after I was feeling a little down and wrote about touching just one person's life, I had a day like today. In all, I had seven clients to come up to me out of nowhere and share how I've helped them with sobriety. I find it totally cool that the Lord had these seven random guys share with me the impact I've made on their lives.

"If you believe, you will receive whatever you ask for in prayer." Matthew 21:22

Almost every night and every time that I'm in a 12-Step meeting, I pray, "God, when they are searching for a 'higher power', please comfort them and show them that You are the Way, the Truth, and the Life." So far through the ministry that I've been doing, I've seen 11 men come to accept the Lord as their personal Savior.

One of the biggest answered prayers was when a particular client told me he'd asked Christ into his heart. While each person I have helped is a blessing from God, this one stands out. We have nothing in common. For starters, he's a card-carrying member of the KKK. I don't think I need to go any further than that.

When he first came to the facility, he wasn't a real nice guy. At the time, I had no idea of his beliefs or where he was coming from. For whatever reason, I just felt led to really minister to and spend time with him. Over the last week he had asked me to give him scriptures to read. Eventually it led to my praying with him, and as I stated before, he accepted Christ into his heart! Amazing.

Working in this field has many ups and downs, peaks and valleys. Basically, it can be a rollercoaster ride. It's really an eye opener to see that God knows exactly what I need to be encouraged. Sometimes it's a month, week, or even a day before the blinders are taken off and I can see God at work. Through it all, He has never failed me.

I wrote last night that it would be nice to see the seeds that I've sown grow. Well today the best type of tree blossomed right before my eyes. Leading someone to Christ is honestly the most rewarding gift one could ever give.

I want to thank all of you who have been praying for me. All of the amazing things that have happened while on this journey are just as much a product of your prayers as anything that I've done. Without the continued support of my fellow believers in Christ, there would be no way I could be so upbeat and joyful in the environment I'm in at work.

Letting Go   October 10th, 2008

Letting go of the past is a complicated subject for me. While I'd like to forget all the horrible things that I've done, sharing it with clients makes my sobriety that much more relevant. For whatever reason, I shared my story with one of the guys and he was absolutely shocked. He thought I was a normal person—not someone who had battled addiction.

It seems that I only open up about my past once or twice a month. For the longest time, I wanted to hide it because of a fear that I'd remember the fun times I used to have. I'd be lying if I said I never enjoyed drinking and doing drugs. Once upon a time I did.

I partied like there was no tomorrow. Do I ever miss my past? Yeah, I do. The only difference is that I also remember the hell I went through. The lifestyle I was living was a miserable existence—always chasing a feeling or high that I could never find.

The life I live today doesn't have the huge highs I had in the past, but at the same time, it doesn't have the valleys that are too painful to explain.

All the previous experiences that I went through are something I can't throw away. They make me the person I am today. The key to dealing with my past is that it's exactly that—my past. Today I live a joyful life in recovery, a life dedicated to helping others and most importantly, a life that has Christ at its center.

God saved me from myself. He has put me in a position where I can share how He has changed my life. What I've had to do is to let go of all the pain and suffering I used to hold onto and accept the love and forgiveness that only Christ can give. It enables me to remember the past and give hope to those who need it.

Someone once asked how I've dealt with all the memories from years past and not want to go back to that lifestyle, how I've let go of all the pain. The answer is simple: I get through every day's temptations through Christ alone. It's in Him that I place my trust and it's only through His strength that I'm able to effectively let go of my past while still remembering what I need to, to help others.

Freedom   October 13th, 2008

Another former client of the place I work relapsed this weekend. He was one of those that I really thought would make it. His transformation over the last two months was miraculous. In fact, I'd just seen him on Friday and was amazed at how well he looked. The sad part was that he accomplished 60 days of sobriety and screwed up the first day he was out of a structured environment.

Freedom is the power or right to act, speak, or think as one wants without hindrance or restraint. For this particular guy, "freedom" allowed him to have one drink which eventually led to another and another. For me, "freedom" is the freedom from drugs and alcohol. I'm no longer in the grasp of a killer disease. By the grace of God, I've been set free and am able to live a joyful life.

Just because I'm a Christian doesn't mean that I no longer have to worry about addictions. What being a follower of Christ means is that I have the best source of strength to rely on to overcome the pitfalls that Satan puts in my way. The master of lies is not happy that I'm sober. In fact, he'll try at all costs to steal away my freedom.

"May the God of hope fill you with all joy and peace as you trust in him, so that you may overflow with hope by the power of the Holy Spirit."
Romans 15:13

Through my reading of the scripture I find all these little nuggets of what the Lord wants me to understand. It's by living a Christ-centered life that I'm able to fully enjoy the freedoms that I never had before. Just because I'm free to make decisions, it's my faith and trust in God that ensures that I don't fall victim to drugs and alcohol.

<u>Marissa</u>   <u>October 14th, 2008</u>

I have an awesome sister. It took 31 years to fully comprehend how special she is. With recent developments at the rehab center, it's abundantly clear that she is one of a kind. Some of the clients have shared how their siblings are reluctant to see them. It seems to be a 75/25 split when it comes to those who are not able to mend fences and those who are able to make things right.

Marissa is in a class of her own. When I finally decided to tell my family that I was an addict, it was less than a month before she was going to get married. I put a damper on one of the most important days of her life. I was a jerk. Two days after she was married, I was put on a plane to rehab. Through it all, she never got angry at me. I later found out that she was crying, trying to figure out what to do about her drug-addicted older brother.

Comparing the two of us is like comparing apples and oranges. I think the only commonality is our parents. She used to say that I had to be adopted. My sister followed all the rules; I was the one who broke rules that were not even in place. Missy was the 4.0 student; I enjoyed spending my high school days at the beach. Despite our many differences, we love each other very much and show it in totally opposite ways.

I'd always tell her high school dates, "Whatever part of your body touches hers, I'll break, cut off, or burn. If I can't do it, I'll find someone who can." Maybe that's why she married Shelby, a martial artist who could destroy me with one hand tied behind his back. While I was rough on her, I tried my best to give her anything she wanted. I spoiled her so badly. I bought her diamond earrings…twice. (She seems to have a problem losing expensive things.)

I think most of the time my sister was embarrassed because of me. She was the princess, and I was the black sheep. Even though she had every right to despise me, she loved me—always praying for me and giving me lame gifts like Christian books and CDs. When I ended up in rehab, she visited me more than anyone in my family. After I completed treatment, she even let me be a houseguest for a week.

The hardest part for me was when she offered me money when I was an inmate at the treatment facility. Never in my life would I have accepted money from her. Coming from a Japanese family, the oldest male taking cash from the younger sister...never. However, that day was a big turning point in my sobriety. I was humbled and saw that I no longer had to have an image; I could just be me. I was broke and wasn't getting any money for a few days. While the amount isn't that important, she gave all that she had.

Today our relationship is the best it's ever been. We call each other at least once a week. It really hasn't changed much. I tease her; she teases me. The one thing that's different from years past is that I call her when I need prayer. The best part is she even calls me for prayer! No matter what, Missy will always be my baby sister ...whether she likes it or not.

Staying Put   October 16th, 2008

"Let us not become weary in doing good, for at the proper time we will reap a harvest if we do not give up." Galatians 6:9

There are times when I want to come home. It's not as often as it was when I first moved up here, but the thought of home-cooked meals, no rent, my old bed, and of course, the dogs make home very appealing.

I was at work today and feeling sorry for myself. A few clients got on my nerves; actually, it was just one. For whatever reason, I had these thoughts that I should just do some martial arts stuff. Yeah, it wasn't my finest moment. Then my genius of a brain thought, "I don't need to put up with this crap; I can go back to the comforts of Hawaii."

It was at this point that I stumbled upon this verse. Regardless of how tired I get, in spite of the stupidity I put up with or the frustration I feel, I need to keep my eyes focused on the job at hand. When the time is right, all the hard work that I'm putting in will one day be worth it. The blessings that will one day occur will be bigger than anything I could ever have dreamed.

Peace   October 21st, 2008

"And the peace of God, which transcends all understanding, will guard your hearts and your minds in Christ Jesus." Philippians 4:7

Peace: freedom from disturbance; quiet and tranquility. The antonyms of peace are agitation, distress, conflict, and war. I work in an environment where peace is rarely found. There are always arguments and situations that need to be defused on a daily basis yet I'm able to find peace here at work.

As ironic as it sounds, the chaos allows me to see the silver lining in events. At times, it's difficult to be peaceful when everything is turned upside down; however, if I keep my eyes on Christ, anything is possible. It's essential that I don't lose my cool; if I do, it can impact the recovery of people around me.

Satan doesn't stop his attacks. In the past, I would've relented and let my emotions get the best of me. Today I realize that most times it's a spiritual attack, and I need to rely on Christ to fight the battles for me. This means I need to stay grounded in the Word and be diligent in my prayer life. The change in results is nothing short of a miracle.

When I was still living a sinful life, it was full of agitation, conflict, and worse yet, I was always at war with someone—usually myself. Luckily, I finally decided to put my trust in God. In turn, He has blessed me with a peace I cannot explain. He has provided for me something that, for 13 years, I never had—peace of mind, body, and spirit. For that I am eternally grateful.

A Tough Prayer   October 24th, 2008

May God bless you with discomfort, easy answers, half truths, and superficial relationships so that in the presence of the living God you may live deep within your heart.

May God bless you with anger at injustice, oppression, and exploitation of people so that in the presence of the living God you may work for justice, freedom, and peace.

May God bless you with tears to shed for those who suffer from pain, rejection, starvation, and war so that in the presence of the living God you may reach out your hand to comfort them and to turn their pain into joy.

And may God bless you with enough foolishness to believe that you can make a difference in this world so that in the presence of the living God you can do what others claim cannot be done. Amen.

This past Sunday the wife of my pastor shared this prayer, A Franciscan Benediction, with the congregation. When she got to the part of shedding tears for those who suffer, I broke down and cried. I like living a comfortable life full of easy answers that don't challenge me. When hearing this prayer, I realized that in order to have that easy life, I don't hear the truth and my relationships are shallow. To get to the bottom of things, tough and honest dialogue is needed.

The last couple of weeks I've not been reading the Word as much as I should. While I continue to read a Proverb a day and have been looking up verses to help the people I work with, I wasn't digging deep to find answers for the issues that I have to deal with personally. Hearing this prayer was a wake-up call that I need to continually challenge myself and not get complacent.

What I'm learning is that Satan is always finding angles to attack me. If I don't stay on top of my game and continue to seek what the Lord has for me, I can get into deep trouble. I noticed that I didn't have that much to write about this week. I think it can be attributed to my recent lack of discipline in Bible reading and prayer. Don't get me wrong, I'm still praying daily; it's just that it's become kind of bland. I was asking for God's help but wasn't thanking Him for the blessings that happen every day.

Prayer isn't just a one-way street where I keep asking and asking and asking for things. When I read the prayer above, it shows me that I should be praying to get closer to Him. While it's a difficult prayer to really believe in, it's one that needs to be prayed.

Humility   October 27th, 2008

"Do nothing out of rivalry or conceit, but in humility consider others as more important than yourselves." Philippians 2:3

There are days when I struggle to embrace this verse. On my own I'm a very selfish and self-centered man. Yet I've been very fortunate to have people in sobriety that live by this scripture, and it reminds me how blessed I am. When I'm finally able to get out of my own head and focus on others, that's when the lights really come on.

There are still times when I'd rather be at the gym or at home watching TV instead of going in early to work. Most days I arrive 1-2 hours before my shift starts just to have time to be around the guys in treatment. What I've noticed is that the days I don't go in early and do something selfish are the days that I feel pretty miserable. The other day, one of the clients commented on how it seems I never leave work....then he thanked me for it. While I never expected anyone to notice, it was nice to hear that I was appreciated.

Almost 20 years ago, I was awarded the JOY Award from my classmates (Jesus 1st, Others 2nd, Yourself last). For whatever reason, I drifted away from being the person who thought of others. In the end, I became cocky and full of myself. While I've lost the innocence of a kid and have been through hell and back, the life I try to live now is being the same person who can put others before myself.

Despite all the effort to be Christ-like, I still fall short. I can still be a punk who is as self-centered as anyone can be. However, now I catch myself and remember what Philippians 2:3 says. As difficult as it can be to swallow my pride and make sacrifices for others, I understand that part of the reason I have sobriety is because others have sacrificed for me.

<u>Prayer</u>   <u>October 28th, 2008</u>

"Watch and pray so that you will not fall into temptation. The spirit is willing, but the body is weak." Matthew 26:41

There are three things that I do daily: pray, read the Bible, and help others. I need to have God watching over me. Even though I'm away from the nightlife scene, Satan is just waiting for me to slip up and fall. Girls, greed, anger, the list goes on.

What is great about my life now is that I know I can't do this on my own. This basic knowledge allows me to give Christ all of my troubles because He can handle anything. There is such relief and blessing in knowing that I have so many people praying for me.

When overcoming addictions, many times the desire to get sober is there, but the problem is that most times the effort required to maintain sobriety is lacking. The one thing that I really emphasize with addicts and alcoholics is prayer. I say that the 12 Steps helped get me sober, but it's my walk (personal relationship) with Christ that keeps me sober.

Overcoming   *October 30th, 2008*

Another one of the guys that I've grown close to is leaving tomorrow. My former roommate relapsed and got kicked out of the last rehab he was in. Grandma is going to be moving to nursing home. This week has been rough.

I was in a funk yesterday. It took a reminder to go the gym and not let the situation get me down. I share with clients all the time about not dwelling on things and turning things over to God. I'm finding out that it's not easy to practice what I preach. The cool thing is that the moment I got out of my head and focused on what was going well was the moment I stopped feeling sorry for myself.

God never promised that life would get easier. He never promised that life would be a bed of roses. What He promised is that He would never leave my side—that when trials and tribulations come, He'll be holding my hand, guiding me each and every step of the way.

Grandma O.   October 31st, 2008

I have an awesome family. While I've shared about my dad, mom, sister, and grandfathers, there are two ladies I've not yet written about—my grandmothers. For the past 13 years I've lived with both of my grandmas. Each is unique in her own way.

The grandmother that I've spent the most time with is Grandma O. I think the most insanely ridiculous stories center around her. She has forgotten who I am at 5 a.m. while walking out of the bathroom and screamed until I reminded her that I was her grandson and lived with her. I think I was more scared than she was. There's also the numerous occasions when she's locked herself out of the house. I guess that's just part of growing old.

It's hard to accept that she's moving into a nursing home. Part of me thinks that if I were to move back home, I could take care of her like I used to. The reality of the situation is that it's just not possible or safe. She has needs that, no matter how much I love her, I cannot fulfill.

Grandma O. was the caretaker of the family—always cooking, cleaning, and going out of her way to make people comfortable. Seeing this once vibrant and outgoing woman becoming more introverted hurts. It's like watching someone disappear in front of my eyes and not being able to do anything about it.

One of the main points of sobriety is learning about acceptance. It's not easy to accept that she'll never be the same—that her better days are behind her. However, if I remember that she in God's care, I really have nothing to worry about.

I can choose to look at the negative or I can focus on the positive. I can think of all the times that on my birthday and on Boy's Day, I could always expect some of Grandma's homemade mochi. When it's cold at night, I can relish the warmth from the blankets she's made. Anytime I eat beef stew, I compare it against her wonderful stew which she has never shared how to make. During the Christmas season when "The Sound of Music" is repeated over and over again, I can remember all the times she made me watch it with her.

It's not easy to deal with her moments of anger, full of hurtful and bewildering words. Yet I know that it's just a by-product of growing old. Observing someone you love slowly drift away into the hands of God can be a painful experience. Or I can choose to see that I have many wonderful memories of her. The light in her eyes may be dimming, but the love she has shown will last forever.

Battle of a Lifetime   November 4th, 2008

One of the reasons I got sober was that I was tired—tired of hiding my addictions, tired of running from my problems, tired of all the lies, overall just tired of who I had become. Living a life of sin had lost its appeal. Even though I had a desire to stop my decadent lifestyle, Satan had me so firmly in his grip that I was unable to be set free.

My freedom from the hellish lifestyle I was in is all because I have Jesus. It's a very simple statement yet so true. I cannot stay sober without my Lord and Savior watching over me daily. On my own I'm weak and vulnerable. I've come to accept that I'm as powerless as a sheep yet blessed to have a shepherd who was willing to die in order for me to live.

My battle with addiction is something I'll have to fight for the rest of my life. I'll never be able to have a beer at a football game. Having a nice red wine to go with my dinner at a fancy Italian Restaurant is out of the question. Visiting the hottest new nightclub is impossible. Ultimately, this is a small price to pay in order for me to live a fruitful and productive life.

Back to Cali   November 12th, 2008

So my trip home is over. I'm at the airport waiting for my flight to depart and I don't want to leave. The last seven days just flew by like a rocket. There's not a single moment that I will forget. The time spent with my family was amazing; the memories made with friends are priceless; and of course, playing with the two doggies will be missed.

Leaving such a beautiful place like Hawaii tears my heart out. The people, food, friendships, and sights will be missed. I think I asked on more than one occasion if I really had to leave. Fortunately for me, the answer from the family was always the same— yes, but you'll be home soon.

My heart will always be in Hawaii. I think the most difficult part was seeing my grandmother in the nursing home today. I just sat and cried. It was a mixture of joy and sadness, hope and despair. The emotions just streamed out of my eyes as I cherished the time with her. I don't know if I'll ever see her again. If there was one overwhelming reason why I didn't want to leave, she was it.

Last week at Thursday night bible study, the topic was Jonah and being obedient. Like Jonah, the human side of me wants to call a taxi right now and head back to Kaimuki; the spiritual side of me knows that I need to go back to California and continue my ministry.

As my dad so eloquently put it on the ride to the airport, "Do you want to end up in the belly of a whale?" I've been disobedient in the past and it led me down a road to self-destruction. This time I will follow God's call even if it is one of the most difficult things I could do.

The Bible never said life would get any easier following Christ. What it does say is that if I'm faithful to God, He'll be faithful to me. Looking back on the last four months that I've been away, I've grown immensely. Following God's will has allowed me to experience life in ways I never dreamed possible. I've come to appreciate all the little things so much more. My love for my family has blossomed into what real agape love is about.

In the end, my time away is only a fraction of my life. I'll miss everything about Hawaii but find comfort in knowing that it will never be that far away. In the meantime, I have my Heavenly Father to thank for the wonderful time I had to spend time with family, friends, and my two dogs.

Being Obedient   November 13th, 2008

I'm back in Cali and amazingly very happy about it. I had thought I'd be missing home. When I went back to work I realized I'd been missed. My fellow co-workers were thrilled to see me yet it was the response from the clients that shocked me.

They all asked how my trip was but also said they had missed me. I cannot count how many of them pulled me to the side and shared how much they were thinking of me while I was away. My being away for seven days seemed like an eternity for some of them. The difference in their attitude and appearance was miraculous.

One client in particular was never attending groups and always sleeping. Today he was a new man—active and being part of the community called rehab. What was even more puzzling was that he remembered me. He wondered when I would be back because I'd been helpful in his journey to sobriety. Looking back, I don't even recall a specific conversation with him; for whatever reason, I'd made an impact on someone and I don't even know how.

I find it fascinating how quickly God showed me that my purpose in life is to be here in California. Less than 24 hours ago, I didn't want to come back to Cali. I was telling my parents that I thought it was a test to see if I was going to be obedient to what God wanted. If there was ever a song that explains what I went through over the last few days....

Trust and Obey by John H. Sammis

Then in fellowship sweet we will sit at His feet,
Or we'll walk by His side in the way;
What He says we will do, where He sends we will go;
Never fear, only trust and obey.
Trust and obey, for there's no other way
To be happy in Jesus, but to trust and obey.

God has been so merciful and loving. He has granted me a new lease on life. Along the way I've come to accept that Satan will always be attacking and finding ways for me to go against what God has in store for me. I was diligent in following what has been put on my heart, and today I can honestly say that I am overjoyed to be back in California. I still miss my family, friends, and dogs yet Christ has given me a peace that I cannot explain, a joy that is overflowing, and sense of purpose once again.

Finally   November 18th, 2008

I met the most fascinating woman today. I was interviewing to be a Big Brother for the church I attend and had to go through an interview process. She had the prettiest smile and a heart of gold. It had been quite a while since I'd had that long of a conversation with a female. In fact, considering the field that I work in, she was the first "normal" person I'd spent time with since I moved.

Yes, it was only an interview and all the questions she asked pertained to the potential volunteer work I would like to do yet it was a welcome change of pace from what I had grown accustomed to. Usually I'm the one asking questions and being interested in what someone has to say. For once I was the one being asked the questions and was allowed to share what my life is about. I guess it didn't hurt that it was a very attractive woman asking.

So what does this have to do with sobriety? I thought that I had lost the ability to communicate effectively with females. Just last night I was texting one of my friends and told her I was actually a shy guy; she called me a liar. The truth of the matter is that in the past, if there was a beautiful woman, it took a few shots of Jack Daniels before I had the courage to say 'hi' for the first time.

While today's discussion wasn't about getting a phone number or asking her out on a date, I finally found that it wasn't liquid courage all these years that allowed me to talk to attractive women. Maybe Briana was right when she told me that I'm not a shy guy. It just took an innocent interview process to realize it.

I guess the last few years I've had this fear of making new friends. I had wrapped my identity around being a nightclubbing maniac. I didn't think I knew how to make new friendships without a shot of alcohol involved. I may not get to volunteer because I may not have enough sobriety time to work with Big Brothers. However, even if I'm not able, I found out something about myself. I can still be the same outgoing and friendly guy sober that I was drunk.

Waiting   November 20ᵗʰ, 2008

Being single is not easy. I would love to have someone during the upcoming holiday season. It would be nice to share time with someone during my days off. In the past, it was very easy to spend time with women but, for whatever reason, that's no longer the case.

For the first four months of my time here in California, it hasn't really bothered me that I don't have the companionship of a woman. I guess it hasn't been an issue because there hasn't been any girl to catch my attention. Well, that has changed. The hard part is that only a few months ago, while fasting and praying, I decided I would no longer chase; instead I would rely on God to "drop her in my lap."

For a while, not chasing after a girl was a breeze; now I'm being put to the test. Part of me wants to go all out and try to spend time with her; however, I know I need to be obedient and fully rely on God.

No Job   November 24ᵗʰ, 2008

I no longer have a job. Due to economic woes, the company I was working for downsized, and since I was the lowest man on the totem pole, I got the ax. Let me start by saying that this was the facility where I had wanted to work, and the shift I was working was ideal. I LOVED working there. It was my dream job.

Despite losing my job, I wasn't angry when I was told the news. In fact, it seems that my co-workers and clients were more upset and bothered than I was. Don't get me wrong, I really miss the clients, co-workers…everything about my job. I really have no clue what I'm going to do next. For the first time in sobriety, I'm lost and confused. The extraordinary part is that by the grace of God, I have a peace about the entire situation.

Usually a situation like this would be a trigger to go back to my old habits. Instead it has provided an opportunity to show others that when Christ is the source of strength, a radical change occurs when handling adverse circumstances. My sponsor was shocked to see how I've been dealing with my emotions and feelings.

I've written in the past that when you rely on Christ, He'll grant you a peace that passes all understanding. Today I can honestly say that I fully comprehend it. Initially I thought, "I can go home." That notion was shot down when both Dad and Mom nixed that idea. I have no idea what I'll be doing without a job. In the interim I've been going to 12-Step meetings, spending time with the guys I sponsor, and working out 2-3 times a day.

There are options out there for me to explore. The hard part for me is following what God wants me to do. I'm asking that all of you pray for me to know the direction I need to go; also pray for "my guys" at the treatment center.

<u>Not My Will</u>   <u>November 25th, 2008</u>

My will got me into rehab; God's will saved my life. I don't know how many times I've used that phrase while working at the treatment center. Whenever one of the guys was thinking of leaving rehab or had a genius idea of how he was going to stay sober without Christ as his "higher power", this was the catch phrase I must have uttered a thousand times.

Well, now I no longer have my dream job—the job I had wanted since I decided that I would one day open a rehab. I was working in the facility that I wanted and on a shift that I thought was ideal. Did you notice that in the previous two paragraphs the word "I" was used 10 times? "God" was used once.

If the statement that God's will saved my life was so important then maybe it's time that His will be my focus. Over the last couple of days there has been a relative calm in my life. Despite the chaos of not knowing what to do next, God has blessed me with a peace of mind that everything is not only going to be okay, but my situation will be even better.

One of the ex-clients asked if I was bitter about being let go. Another guy asked if I was angry. In essence, every question that's been thrown my way has been about whether I'm going home, if I have resentment, or what I'm going to do next. In every situation, I've been able to say, "I don't know what I'll be doing, but God is in control, and that's fine by me."

It's not easy to sit here and type that I have no clue where or when I'll be working next. However, there is great relief knowing that God is in control and will answer all my prayers in His time. It's a perfect opportunity for me to fully comprehend the Fruit of the Spirit. I love that I had the chance to work at such an awesome facility. There's joy in knowing that God's hand is at work. I have peace even though in the eyes of the world, my situation is a mess. I will have patience while I wait upon the Lord. I will show kindness to those less fortunate than I. I will demonstrate goodness by showing others that when Christ is the source of strength, it's still possible to be a positive person in spite of adversity. I will show faithfulness by believing that this has all happened for a reason. Others will witness my humility when they watch me lose a job for the first time and not be bitter. I've exercised self-control in difficult circumstances in that I've never once had the urge to do something stupid.

I Miss My Guys   November 26th, 2008

I miss my guys. Deep down inside, my heart aches to be back at work. Even though the pain is still there, I know God has His hand on my life and that I need to accept things. There is both confusion and frustration in my current predicament. However, in the quiet moments of the day, when I'm not pondering what to do next, there's a peace about it that I can't put into words. It's these blessed moments of clarity that allow me to keep my head on straight.

For whatever reason, I decided to attend a meeting tonight. Well, part of it was that I would be able to see the clients; I knew where they would be. Anyway, one of the guys pulled me aside and thanked me for saving his life. At the time, I really didn't put much thought into it. Later another client came up to me and said the same thing. One of the reasons I'd wanted to get into this field was because Tait, one of my roommates in rehab who had committed suicide. I dedicated my sobriety to helping prevent another person from ending up like he did.

Tonight's events made me realize that I'd made a difference in someone's life. When it came time to share in the meeting, I felt led to talk about how God had granted me a peace about being laid off because some of the men were having a hard time with my being let go. Toward the end of my speech, I said how much I miss my guys and how I love each one of them. In unison some of my guys yelled out, "We love you, Jon."

Even though my intent was to assure them that I'd be okay, they showed me a level of love that touched my heart more than they will ever know. After I finished, one of the guys sitting next to me put his arm around me and thanked me for everything. In the end, every single one of the clients came up, gave me a big hug, and wished me well. The words of encouragement were exactly what I had wanted to give to them yet I was the one who was filled with hope, love, and appreciation.

I still don't know when or where I'll be working. All I do know is that God has blessed me more love than I could ever imagine. I thought that I was the one helping addicts and alcoholics and in the end, the addict that was getting help was me!

Finding the Silver Lining   November 28th, 2008

Finding that silver lining through dark clouds is usually something I have to really search for. However, it seems that ever since I've been laid off, the silver lining is so obvious I'd have to be a complete moron to not see it.

It's been almost a week since the dreaded day that I was laid off. I use the word "dreaded" with a grain of salt. As dreadful as losing a job can be, today I can say there's a part of me that's actually rejoicing that I'm currently unemployed.

Before some of you email, call, or text me to say that I'm out of mind, let me clarify by saying that it sucks not knowing how rent will be paid in two months. There's a fear that this will be a reason for me to come home. Not having a steady income causes me to wonder if I've not been obedient, and I'm confused at what to do next.

That being said...God is great. Over the last week, I think I've connected and ministered on a deeper level than I ever had over the last three months combined. Today I was able to volunteer at my former place of employment and share how awesome God is even though times may look rough. I've picked up two more people to sponsor that, had I still been working, I would not be able to sponsor.

The most telling and amazing experience happened tonight. It's moments like these that remind me that I'm where God wants me to be. I was blessed to have Thanksgiving dinner at a sober living house where a number of ex-clients are staying. While the food was fantastic and the feeling of being a part of a family was well needed, something happened along the way that solidified my conviction that Cali is home for now.

There was a young man there who will be leaving to go back home in less than 24 hours. While he wasn't a client when I was working, he was there when I shared my testimony six months ago. The crazy part is that he remembered me. I really have no clue how our conversation started, but what transpired over the course of our talk was exactly the confirmation I needed.

We talked about numerous things. I got more spiritual in my discussion with him than I have with anyone in a long time. In the end, I asked if I could pray for him, not expecting anything in return. After I was done, he prayed for me and opened my eyes about how God works in mysterious ways that I will never comprehend.

This young man prayed in such a way that I knew it was God using him to speak directly to me. Every single fear, thought, question, everything that I'd been doubting about my staying in California, was answered. Once again, I thought I was helping someone and in the end that person was helping me.

I sit here in cold weather, 2,500 miles from home, without a job, with no family anywhere close, and I am so very thankful. I'm thankful that God has placed me where I need to be. I'm thankful for an astounding group of new "family" and friends. Most importantly, I'm thankful that God loves me with so much compassion and grace and continues to bless me in miraculous ways.

For all who are reading this, I have a prayer request. Pray that Grant finds his place in this world, that all the fears and questions he has are answered in God's time, and that he is able to discern exactly what God has in store for him. This young man touched my life tonight and reminded me that following God's will is never easy yet with Christ as the source of strength, miracles happen.

Bad Day   December 1st, 2008

    I don't really feel like writing. It seems that chaos is the word that best describes life now. Not really mine but those around me. Being in a positive frame of mind is a constant challenge when negative things overwhelm me. I need to remind myself that others are watching how I'm handling adversity.

    Tonight I was feeling sorry for myself. I was asking, "Why me? When is it going to be my turn?" Pretty much being a selfish, self-centered crybaby. God gave me a swift kick-in-the-butt when, in the middle of my pity party, I got a phone call that one of the guys I'd taken to church today relapsed. I was just with the guy two hours earlier and he had seemed perfectly fine. Now he's going to be kicked out and probably have to live in a motel.

    Due to my current state of mind—being without a job, far from home, and questioning what I'm doing here—I was initially inclined to think I was a failure at helping in recovery. For whatever reason, I re-read what one of my pastors back home said in an email, that what I am doing reminds him of the apostle Paul. I refocused my thoughts that it really has nothing to do with me. All Paul did was let others know what "truth" is; it was up to the Ephesians, Philippians, Colossians, Thessalonians, etc. to decide if they would follow Christ.

I don't come close to what Paul did in Biblical times yet he's given me an example to follow. The man once known as Saul who persecuted Christians eventually was transformed into one of the greatest evangelists of his time. I can only hope to do a fraction of what he did.

I usually tell others that they need to put just as much effort into sobriety as they put in addiction. For me, this was my turn to show that it does work. A few years ago, if I was having such a crappy time in life, I would've hit the bars or called a drug dealer. Instead of going out and doing something stupid, I decided to sit and write this entry and because of it I'm way more at peace with my current situation and grateful for what I have.

Ego Sucks   December 2nd, 2008

Today started off horribly. Okay, not really horribly; nightmarish would probably be a better term. I was under the impression that I'd be receiving my last paycheck today; I was wrong. It's coming on the 15th. To make matters worse, rent was due today. Since I'm pretty good with numbers, I was able to calculate that I still had enough to cover the rent, but my bank balance would be below the minimum and I'd have to pay a fee. Considering that I'm jobless, extra fees are not my best friend.

I was very apprehensive about going to my bank and really starting to stress out about the whole thing. I decided to swing by the house and change into my workout clothes so I could work out all my frustrations after doing my banking. To my surprise, there was mail from home. Grandma had sent me a Thanksgiving gift. By the grace of God, earlier last week my sister had also sent me a check to help out. With the deposit and withdraw for my rent, I was $3 in the clear.

Early this morning I was a basket case; later in the afternoon I was really relieved, and tonight I sit here totally at peace, realizing that God always provides. Part of me wishes I'd really thought things through. I guess I needed to be reminded that if I focus on the problem and not the solution, I become a scared lunatic. I kept thinking, "What am I going to do? Where am I going to get more money? How am I going to survive?" Once again the word "I" got me into trouble. The crazy part is that my butt is only in trouble when I have an ego...Easing God Out.

Prayer & Peace   December 3rd, 2008

Peace. Other terms for peace include, calm, restfulness, quiet, solitude, tranquility, harmony, and serenity. For 13 years of my life, I can honestly say that peace was not a part. I was always fighting someone, hostile to loved ones, at war with everyone and everything including myself. Today that is not the story. I can have peace in the midst chaos.

Earlier tonight someone asked me to pray for him and stated that I say good prayers. At the time it really didn't affect me yet as I type this entry I'm reflecting on why I'm able to be at peace with everything that's going on. The answer is very simple: prayer.

I've noticed that I start every prayer in the same way. "Gracious Heavenly Father, thank you for today." Maybe it's because I'm so repetitive that it's been ingrained in my brain that God is gracious, and I give thanks to Him at all times regardless of the situation.

Another common occurrence when I pray is that even though there may be a problem that I pray about, I thank God for it. Why? Because in His infinite wisdom there's a reason for the trial that's in front of me. I can be a real stubborn idiot, and most of the time I need the obstacle put in front of me to fully understand what God's trying to teach me.

For so many years of my life, whenever a complication arose, drugs and alcohol were my answer. Ultimately, that took me down a very dark and dangerous road that I'm very fortunate to have survived. Now when those same misfortunes occur I turn to the One who has all the answers…Christ.

Amazing Grace   December 4th, 2008

Amazing Grace by John Newton

Amazing Grace, how sweet the sound,
That saved a wretch like me.
I once was lost but now am found,
Was blind, but now I see.

I must have sung this song hundreds of times and never fully grasped its meaning. When I finally gave my life and will to God, I was able to truly appreciate this wonderful hymn. It's only by the grace of God that I can sit here today and share my story of hope. For so many years I was a lost soul searching for a reason to live.

Usually the paths I took led nowhere. Okay, let's be honest: for many years I was a blind fool stumbling through life without a clue where to go. I was a drunk, selfish, self-centered drug addict who eventually hurt everyone I encountered. There were broken relationships and pain all around me. Many times I was the cause for the destruction that was left behind.

Eventually I was just tired of living life in a drunken and drug-laden stupor and found that God's grace was still there. In reality, it was always there; I was just blinded by Satan's lies and unable to see that God's hand was right next to me waiting for me to grab hold of it. When I finally embraced His mercy and love, that was when I realized how awesome God is.

The Lord has promised good to me.
His word my hope secures.
He will my shield and portion be
as long as life endures.

In sobriety I have learned that as long as I put my trust in Him, miracles can and will happen. What keeps me in line is that most times it doesn't happen when I want it; usually it's when I least expect it. Through all the trials and tribulations I've had, every time I rely on Christ, great and wonderful things happen; when I try to dictate and control things, disaster happens.

Even though it's finally gotten through my thick skull that I need to give everything over to God's care, I still make mistakes. The best part is that it's becoming a less frequent occurrence. I just need to remember that He will be my shield and provide all that I need as long as life endures.

Obedience   *December 5th, 2008*

Being obedient is not easy. In all seriousness, obedience is something I still struggle with today. I want to do things my way, make my own rules, and listen to no one but myself. Despite knowing that my way is going to get me into trouble, I still do it. A stubborn pain-in-the-butt is what I can be.

One of the best things I've learned in sobriety is that when I'm listening to what God has to say, great things happen. The times

I try to do things on my own have become fewer and fewer. In return, my life has been blessed way beyond anything I could've done on my own. When I gave my life and will over to Christ, He rewarded me beyond my wildest imagination.

In 2009, I'm being considered to be interviewed on a radio program that's broadcast nationwide. The desire to share my story with as many people as possible was one of the reasons I created my website. Never in my wildest dreams did I think I'd be able to reach so many people as this opportunity will present. There' no doubt that this amazing opportunity would not have happened had I not been obedient to God in making some of the decisions I've made recently.

"Do not repay evil with evil or insult with insult, but with blessing, because to this you were called so that you may inherit a blessing. For whoever would love life and see good days must keep his tongue from evil and his lips from deceitful speech, He must turn from evil and do good; he must seek peace and pursue it. For the eyes of the Lord are on the righteous and his ears are attentive to their prayer, but the face of the Lord is against those who do evil."
1 Peter 3:9-12

If I'd stayed in Hawaii and neglected to follow God's call, if my attitude when dealing with being laid off had been negative and full of anger, if I had reverted back to my old way of thinking, this remarkable opportunity would never have happened.

In some cases I share how life is rough and I ponder why things happen. Well, this entry is just an illustration that when I'm obedient to God, jaw-dropping events happen. There is no question in my mind that none of the recent extraordinary things would have occurred if I'd tried to do things on my own.

Praise Where Praise is Due   December 8th, 2008

"If anyone speaks he should do it as one speaking the very words of God. If anyone serves, he should do it with the strength God provides, so that in all things God may be praised through Jesus Christ. To Him be the glory and the power forever and ever. Amen." 1 Peter 4:11

This past week I've been the beneficiary of so many words of praise and things that could blow my ego into the size of a football field. It's great to hear words to boost my self-esteem. Through it all, though, I've maintained that it really isn't anything that I've done; it's only possible to do what I've been doing through Christ.

Someone said that I speak words of wisdom. Well, I know where I get those words—by reading the Word of God. I gladly help others; it's the servanthood that I learned from Jesus' example. Ultimately, everything that I'm doing is a reflection of my personal relationship with Christ.

The fact that I'm still sober is a testament to the power of prayer and making an effort to become closer to God. In my addictions, following Christ was the farthest thing from my mind. If ever I was praised for anything, I'd let it go to my head. Luckily for me, I was able to reconnect to my roots and the proper source of strength.

Forget Perfection   December 9th, 2008

Earlier today I received an email from Pastor Kaala Souza. He just started a new website called soulfit.kaala.com, a site that helps get our souls in shape. The first "exercise" he assigned was to write what we're thankful for. Having an attitude of gratitude has allowed me to really appreciate what I have today.

It's not easy to find reasons to be grateful when times are rough. The lesson I've learned is that if I decide to focus on the difficulties, I lose sight of the many blessings that are around. Our society makes it seem that money, power, and fame are things that make us who we are. What I know now is that money comes and goes, power is an illusion, and fame is not what it's cracked up to be.

Today I can say that the gifts from Christ are more valuable than gold. I cannot put a price tag on love, joy, and peace. The "power" that I get from God allows me to have patience and strength to be kind and good to others. Humility and self-control definitely do not go hand-in hand with fame.

Having the Fruit of the Spirit as part of my life is something I hold onto dearly. While I strive to live by it daily, I still fail. What I've come to appreciate is that all God asks from me is effort. One of my new catch phrases is, "Forget perfection, strive for excellence." I will never ever be perfect, but if I remain faithful and thankful to God, excellent results will come my way.

Price to Pay   December 16th, 2008

Life has been great, and at the same time, very difficult. So much has happened there's no way to know where to start. There's the pending job opportunity that I'm not totally at peace with. With Dad being here for a week, there are stories of how it's great to have a relationship with family. Big Brothers finally gave its approval, and I met up with my Little Brother. And of course, there's just life in general.

Sometimes I get so caught up in what's going on around me that I forget I need my own quiet time to connect with Christ. My recent lack of time with God has affected me negatively. I'm on edge, not at peace, flying off the handle. All of this is probably stressing my folks back home. In essence, I've made a mess of things; yet God has blessed me with something I do not take for granted—sobriety.

Since being laid off, I've decided to keep busy and go out of my way to help others. The reward of helping others has been beyond my imagination. I've met new friends, been drawn closer to old friends, and signed up for fresh opportunities. Overall great things have happened yet there's a void I cannot deny—my personal relationship with Christ is not as strong as it once was.

When I was working, my routine was something I'd grown very accustomed to; however, with all this free time the routine is no longer there. Instead of taking more time to focus on what God wants me to do, I decided to just run full steam ahead with what I thought was right.

Now I have too many responsibilities, a job offer that I never really put time into praying over, and a month of choices that were not Christ-driven. The end result? A very stressful existence. I got caught up in my will, and now I'm paying for it.

The funny thing is that this whole time I thought I was doing what was best—being a servant, sacrificing my time to help others, and not focusing on the negatives in life. While they are all positive, in the end the one thing that was neglected was Jesus. It just goes to show that it's not what I do, it's how I do it.

In the end, I know that if I turn everything over to God, things will sort themselves out. There's a price to pay for my mistakes. I may have to let people down and not go through with some of the things I thought I would do; nonetheless, if I focus on God's will, everything will work out for the better.

Comfort   December 17th, 2008

> *"Praise be to the God and Father of our Lord Jesus Christ, the Father of compassion and the God of all comfort, who comforts us in all our troubles, so that we can comfort those in any trouble with the comfort we ourselves have received from God. For just as the sufferings of Christ flow over into our lives, so also through Christ our comfort overflows." 2 Corinthians 1:3-5*

Life is hard right now. I'm still clueless in what I'll be doing for a living. I see people struggling to make ends meet, and I witness the utter despair that people are going through right now. The economy sucks, and I realize that there is nothing I can do about it. Well, I can pray and turn everything over to God.

If I choose to focus on the negative, I'd be deeply depressed. The list above is really just a snippet of what could've been listed. The fact is that it doesn't matter what's wrong. If I'm a believer in Christ, I need to turn EVERYTHING over to Him—not just bits and pieces of my life, but absolutely everything.

It's not easy to praise God when things are rough; the easy thing is to get caught up in the craziness and take out my frustrations on others. It would be simple to wallow in my self-pity and try to fix things; however, that's not what God wants from me. He wants me to trust in Him and to allow Him to comfort me and supply my needs.

Being a Christian is not about living the easy life. Sometimes I think God purposely allows difficult times so I'll draw closer to Him. He makes mountains of problems turn into little speed bumps. The inevitable blessing that comes from God can only happen if I get out of the way and let Him take care of it.

Simple Suggestions   December 18th, 2008

It was a very cold and rainy day here in Southern California. Despite the external gloominess, I had a great day. There's nothing specific that dictated why today was so awesome; it just was. I could share about how one of the guys I sponsor had adversity and found a way to overcome it without the thought of drugs or alcohol. I could talk about my meeting with a pastor that shed some light on my current situation. Then there's the fact that someone I've been talking with accepted Christ.

Regardless of what's going on around me, when this man told me he had asked Christ into his heart, that trumped everything. A broken and angry guy just a few days ago was now someone seeking to serve the Lord. Now, that is a miracle!

Recently I've formulated a few suggestions for the people I sponsor. First, I tell them to write down all the people they love and why. I ask them to read it over each morning so they recognize what they have to be thankful for. Next, I suggest that they read Titus 3, Romans 5, and Philippians 2. There are also the daily tasks of reading the Bible, praying, and being of service.

Do I think that this is the cure-all for all addicts and alcoholics? Nope. What I do know is that what I wrote above is what helps me to stay sober and has also been beneficial to those who are around me.

Seeking Wisdom   December 19th, 2008

I know I should be writing something but at the moment I'm drawing a blank. Actually, this is my fourth attempt tonight at trying to write. The previous three have been deleted, so please bear with me if this is not one of my finest entries.

It seems that my mind is moving at a million miles per hour with not much substance behind it. Random thoughts of whether my Dallas Cowboys will make the playoffs, when I'll go back home, family issues, how the guys that I sponsor are doing, when I'll be able to work again . . .

Despite the obscene amount of thoughts flowing through my head, I still feel there's something I need to share. I don't think I've ever taken this long to write; there's a part of me that just wants to quit and watch some TV and go to bed. As I sit here typing, I'm searching for a reason to write but have so much on my mind that I can't seem to put my finger on what I'm supposed to blog about.

Now that I've wasted three paragraphs on absolutely nothing, I got it. Many times in life there's something that needs to be done yet I don't know what it is. I know that my goal is to help people in sobriety and recently I've been struggling with how I should do it. Is it by becoming a drug and alcohol counselor? Opening a rehab center in Hawaii? Becoming a pastor with an emphasis on people in recovery? Is it just writing this blog? Will I be someone to speak at churches?

I think the randomness of my earlier thoughts are ways that I avoid what's really bothering me. I've tried to escape from the decisions that are important by covering them up with nonsense. I've been running from what is really the issue that I should be dealing with. I'm reminded of this verse:

"If any of you lacks wisdom he should ask God, who gives generously to all without finding fault, and it will be given to him." James 1:5

Please be in prayer for me because I'm still seeking what God wants me to do. I've been praying about where I need to be headed and still have not gotten an answer. So I guess I'm asking you to pray that I'll have patience to wait on His answer, wisdom to know where God is leading me, and courage to follow His plan.

It Takes Effort   December 22nd, 2008

I got re-hired at my old workplace. It may only be a two-month stint; nonetheless, it's something that brings me joy. What makes things even better is the response from those around me. For some of them this was tangible evidence that prayer works.

On the flip side, I'm now having problems with the guys I sponsor. Reminders that the disease of alcoholism and addiction is cunning, baffling, and deceiving are now rearing their ugly heads right in front of my eyes. No matter how much I try, their lack of concern and unwillingness to do the things necessary to stay sober confounds me.

It's hard to see a train wreck waiting to happen and being utterly powerless to stop it. One guy has this genius idea of not going to meetings, not going to church, not reading his Bible, and not going to work, and he thinks that there's nothing wrong with that. That's insane. He would rather spend time with his girlfriend and watch TV.

Stupid does not even begin to explain what I think of the situation. Instead of being a man and taking ownership of his recovery, he chooses to blame others and say that he's not being shown respect. Sorry, respect is earned.

Having watched him make stupid choice after stupid choice for the last two days has started to drain me. He's still sober but I honestly have no clue for how much longer. That's the sad part. He was doing so well, doing all the right things, and making progress. Now he seems to think he has all the answers. I don't think for a moment that I have all the answers, but I've seen others attempt to do what he's currently doing, and the result is disaster.

This experience with him has humbled me. I thought I could be a great sponsor and make a difference. The truth of the matter is that, without Christ as the foundation, nothing really matters. Part of me thinks I've failed, that somewhere I screwed up. After some deep reflection, though, I know I did my best. It's not my fault when someone is not willing to work at sobriety.

Which brings me to my main point. Sobriety is like anything you want in life. Whether it's a personal relationship with Christ, a big house on the lake, money, nice body, etc., it takes work, hard work. For anyone reading this blog who has a goal, any goal, know that without effort, it will never happen.

Reminder   December 23rd, 2008

Shame, guilt, embarrassment, anger, hate, loathing, fear, uncertainty, hopelessness, etc. are a few reasons that I used drugs and alcohol. During my addiction I was enslaved by the lies that Satan told me. There were some nights that I was so depressed it didn't matter how much I drank or the amount of drugs I consumed; I was still miserable. I felt unloved and unworthy of anything of value.

The pain and suffering that were part of my hedonistic lifestyle actually drove me back to using. I thrived on the pain as an excuse to continue abusing my body. The craziest part was that not only did the drugs and alcohol NOT numb me but they made the situation worse.

In the last six months of my stupidity, I sneezed out a chunk of cartilage from my nose; I sliced open the bottom of my foot; blacking out and waking up on the bathroom floor was common; a constant craving for drugs consumed my life; I would hear voices. In the end, I was so paranoid that I thought the police had tapped my phone and were out to get me. The most genius part? I still did drugs and drank Jack Daniels like it was going out of business.

I share all of this because one of the guys I sponsor relapsed. It breaks my heart that he was unable to overcome his demons and stay sober. This entry was just for me. A reminder that once upon a time I was just as lost and confused as he is right now. All I can do is love him like Christ loves me and continue to pray for him.

"Do not judge or you too will be judged. For in the same way you judge others; you will be judged, and with the measure you use, it will be measured to you." Matthew 7:1-2

The Answer   December 24th, 2008

After yesterday's blog, I was asked how someone helps a person who is in recovery. For those of you who are "normies" (not an addict or an alcoholic), you first must understand what it's like to be one who struggles with drugs and alcohol. The best way I can explain it is to turn the stove on, put your hand on it, watch your flesh burn, feel the excruciating pain, see your hand start to blister, go to bed, and the next morning repeat everything over again.

It is an insane way of living life, but that's the closest explanation of what this disease is like—psychotic. What I'm trying to get across is that there is nothing any human being can do to help someone battling addiction; only God can remove the desire to abuse drugs and alcohol.

Fortunately, I've been able to have God wipe clean all the crazy thoughts of my past. Today I can sit here with all the chaos that Satan can throw at me and be able to live a joyful life in sobriety. The only way this is possible is by praying daily, reading the Bible daily, and helping others who are struggling with addiction.

The answer to the question first stated in this entry is prayer, unconditional love, and more prayer. There is nothing that anyone could've done for me to make me sane. It is by the grace of God that I am alive today. For all those who read this blog, I humbly ask that you be in prayer for those I come across on a daily basis.

If you don't know what to pray, that's okay. Here's a sample of what I say when I'm praying for those in recovery: "Gracious Heavenly Father, thank You so much for today. Thank You for the opportunity to come before you. Please bless _____. Show them Your amazing love. Comfort them in their time of need. Grant a peace which surpasses all understanding. Your love and mercy are priceless. Allow Your will to be a part of their lives. Show them that You are an almighty and caring God. Remove all the fear and guilt that separates them from Your love. Bless them in all they do, show them what Your will is for their lives. Thank You for loving them in their broken and scared state of mind because it's only through You that they have redemption. In Your precious Son Jesus' name I pray. Amen."

Sometimes I'm Still Stupid   December 29th, 2008

Yesterday my serenity level was at zero. Megan would say that my serenity level was at negative 100. Yes, yesterday sucked. If there's anyone to blame for my crap, it's me. There's no reason I should've been in a bad place. I spent most of the day preparing a meal for 30 people at the sober living house. I was able to have the people I sponsor helping me. In other words, it should've been a great day; instead, I allowed stupid thoughts to ruin an otherwise great day.

Fortunately for me, I spent time with my Little Brother from the Big Brother Program today. Here's a kid who's on the same drugs that the people in rehab are on. He hasn't seen his mother for almost three years. When I showed up 10 minutes late, he thought I'd brushed him off. For so many years he's felt unloved and unwanted. At one point during our conversation he stated that he was "bad" and that was why no one wants him around. That couldn't be farther from the truth; his mom is a drug addict who has lost custody of him.

After three hours with this young man, I realized that I was just being a loser. I actually don't remember the worst part of yesterday. The funny part was that a few weeks ago I was talking with Megan and told her about HALT, never making decisions when Hungry, Angry, Lonely, or Tired. For whatever reason, I was so tired and didn't catch myself slipping into a bad frame of mind, lonely being away from home, and angry that I wasn't getting the respect I thought I deserved. Stupid, stupid, stupid.

Rest Needed   December 30th, 2008

Pooped, exhausted, sick, tired, overwhelmed... Combine all those feelings and what you end up with is me. I don't think I've had one day off in the last five weeks. I may not be working but I'm being of service and probably over-extending my physical, mental, and emotional limits. I find it kind of funny, but yesterday my Dad told me to take a day off. Never in a million years during my time as a lazy drug addict and alcoholic would I ever have expected my Dad to tell me to take it easy.

There's this burning desire in my soul to be helping others. From the moment I wake up 'til the time I go to bed, I try my best to be a light in the dark world of recovery. What I fail to remember is that without rest, my light becomes barely a flicker. The only time I spend on myself is when I go to the gym, and even that has suffered of late.

My body is run down and I've been battling a cold for almost two weeks. My emotional health is drained to the point that the smallest irritation sets me off. I don't even want to talk about my spiritual health since my serenity level is at zero. The best part of my life today? I know how to deal with this. I need to take a day off and let it be my "Sabbath Day."

I've focused so much on events—taking out my Little Brother, working with the guys I sponsor, volunteering at the rehab, going to 4-5 meetings/church services, etc. that I have lost focus on what's important—my personal relationship with Christ. The crazy part is that I just wrote about this same topic last week. I guess it just goes to show you that I'm still an idiot at times.

As the New Year rolls around and resolutions are made, here are two that I will be setting that I dare not screw up. I will devote one hour a day for just me and God, whether that be listening to praise and worship music, reading the Bible, praying, or writing in a private journal. I will also set aside one full day a week that I will do nothing but rest, relax, and enjoy life, alone or with others, doing something not based on recovery stuff.

I've been so wrapped up in doing "stuff" that I've forgotten what the whole purpose of sanitizeyoursoul.org is all about: living a joyful life in sobriety. I'm not saying I've not enjoyed anything over the last month; it's just that in order for me to be an effective person, I need to be a healthy person.

Prayer for the New Year   *December 31ˢᵗ, 2008*

This being the last entry of this year, I thought I'd do something a little different. What is written below is my prayer for the New Year. Some may think of it as a New Year's resolution; I think of it as a way for all who read my blog to have something in mind while praying for me and my ministry.

"Gracious Heavenly Father, thank You for today. I am so unworthy of Your mercy and grace yet have been the recipient of Your unquestionable love. You alone are worthy of praise. Your compassion and understanding show how awesome You are. You give me the strength needed to overcome all the obstacles Satan puts in my way. Your wisdom while helping those struggling with addiction goes beyond my wildest imagination. Despite my insecurities and fears, Your powerful loving arms wrap themselves around me and allow me to defeat the king of lies.

"In the upcoming year I ask for knowledge and courage to follow the path You've laid before me. Your authority over all things will allow me to climb mountains that seem impossible to scale. Bless those You have put in my path, allow Your love to shine through the example You ask of me.

"Thank You, Lord, for loving someone as broken and unfit as I. On my own, I am doomed to fail, but with Christ on my side I can accomplish miraculous things. Thank You for the opportunity to shed light on a dark and lonely world. Thank you, Father, for Your patience with me. Thank You for the wonderful life You have blessed me with. Thank You for the undeniable gift of salvation that

Christ gave me when He died on the cross for all my sins. In Your precious Son Jesus' name, I pray. Amen."

New Creation   January 2nd, 2009

"So from now on we regard no one from a worldly point of view. Though we once regarded Christ in this way, we do so no longer. Therefore, if anyone is in Christ, he is a new creation; the old is gone, the new has come." 2 Corinthians 5:16-17

It's not easy to change. For quite some time I thought all my old habits had disappeared. Drinking and doing drugs are not even a thought in my mind. I may have a dream about the white powdery stuff every couple of months, but waking up in a cold sweat dreading a relapse is a great reminder of why I'll never go back.

With that out of the way, I have to admit that I'm still weak in some areas. For those of you who know me from back home, you shouldn't have to think that hard...women. My decision making concerning the opposite sex has not changed one bit. I can have three choices in front of me, and even if they all looked the same, I'd be attracted to the one that I probably wouldn't want to take home to Mom and Dad.

It totally baffles me. It's like I have a dunce cap on my head each and every time I get interested in someone. The good ones seem to have only a passing interest, the 50/50 females get my attention, and the ones that just scream "stay away"? Well, those are the ones I fall for. I never really understood why until I went to a meeting tonight.

The speaker shared that, for whatever reason, people in recovery walk away from the good and run to the bad. I guess there's a part of my brain that, I have to admit, is drawn to the naughty side of life. Considering I'm a recovering drug addict and alcoholic, that shouldn't come as a shock to anyone. What was shocking for me was that I thought I'd left behind all the stupid decision making.

God must be having a good ol' time in heaven chuckling a little bit at my predicament. I was willing to turn over my addictions but obviously thought I could hold onto parts of my party past. Luckily for me, I caught on and decided to actually follow the "stay away" flashing lights. Who knows, that special someone may just fall in my lap tomorrow? If she doesn't, that's fine by me because on my own I'm in trouble, but if I choose to wait upon the Lord, great things happen.

Staying in the Moment   January 5th, 2009

For whatever reason, the theme of "just be" has permeated a ton of my discussions recently. It's a hard concept to explain, but something that my martial arts instructor taught me when I had a few months of sobriety time. Relax, it's not some new age meditating thing. He had noticed that I was constantly text messaging or fiddling with something and had asked me to "just be in the moment."

He was so right. Despite being in the presence of others, my mind was always racing—thinking of something, someone, or some other place. The term "chattering monkeys" was his reminder phrase whenever he caught me drifting off into space. In recovery, I've found that many of the people I come in contact with have the same problem I have—these stupid monkeys that just won't shut up.

The reason that I fidget or text message when others are around is usually because I'm uncomfortable with what's going on. When I let my mind wander, crazy thoughts spin in my head. I get cranky, moody, frustrated, lonely, irritable, etc.; in other words, I'm heading down the path to doing something stupid. For others, the feeling of being uncomfortable pushes them back to addiction.

I've learned that if I can stay in the moment and deal with everything going on around me, eventually the "monkeys" get quiet and I'm able to handle whatever comes my way. There are some little techniques I've found useful in silencing the noise. If I'm alone, I do breathing exercises but never in public because they may think I'm nuts.

The best activity is to pray and ask God to remove any unclean thoughts that may hinder living a Godly life. Going to the gym, listening to my iPod, working out for 45 minutes, or reading a few scriptures that I have highlighted in my iPhone does the job also. It's a diverse list but it works for me.

Are You Ready?   January 6th, 2009

Are you ready? Are you tired of waking up in the morning feeling like a truck just ran over you? Do the days seem to blur into weeks and the months into years? Is drinking and doing drugs just something you do because that's all you know to do? Does the term "relationship" extend only as far as your drug dealer and bartender? Have you ever poured hydrogen peroxide into your sinus cavity because you think it will clean out all the blood and allow you to do more cocaine?

If you answered "yes" to any of these questions, you may want to consider getting clean and sober. Twenty months ago to the day I answered "yes" to each and every one of those questions. I was a very sick and twisted individual. The last question I mentioned didn't happen just once, and to answer any of you who may think it hurt, the pain of doing that is indescribable. It's also part of the reason I still have sinus issues to this day and am missing part of my septum.

Drug addiction and alcoholism sucks. The fun ended long before I ever got help. Excuses for not seeking treatment could fill pages and pages. The utter despair and hopelessness that ruled my life nearly killed me. A path straight to hell was paved, and I was on the fast track to living the rest of my life as a total loser.

Did my recovery happen overnight? I guess the answer is both yes and no. God relieved me from the obsession to snort things up my nose, smoke the green herb that I loved, and the desire to drown my sorrows in Jack Daniels after the first time I prayed for Him to do so. However, the process of learning to live without all the garbage is very slow and gradual.

If you're considering this thing called sobriety, give it a try. That feeling you had when you first got high will elude you forever. The blackouts from too much alcohol and waking up naked on the bathroom floor will cease to exist. Having the taxi service on speed dial because you're afraid of getting a D.U.I won't be an issue. Wondering how to get more cash because the drug dealer doesn't accept a credit card won't be how you spend most of your time.

A peace which has disappeared from your life will one day reappear. Fulfilling and worthwhile friendships will be within reach. The opportunity of helping others is no longer just a thought; it's something you can do. Finding joy in the simplest things, such as a two-year-old running up to say he loves you, is possible. The ability to wake up each morning excited to see what God has in store is priceless. Most importantly, you'll finally be able to go to sleep with a clear conscience and realize how awesome life is.

What Sobriety Brings   January 7th, 2009

Accountability, honesty, trust, keeping commitments, listening to others, being a servant, showing up on time…that's just the beginning. These are the things I now have in my life. Last night I did some major stretching and woke up with a pain in my leg that made me want to stay in bed. The only thing was that I had a commitment. In the past, I would have flaked out and been a no-show.

How I want to live my life today won't allow me to be a space cadet. Some of you are waiting for the great words of wisdom or the amazing experience that I had at that meeting. The truth of the matter is that nothing I gave input on was done and essentially, I was just another body in a room full of ideas. Even though I have a background in planning events and those in the room had zero experience, my suggestions fell on deaf ears. For me, I think that was the best possible thing to happen.

As someone who battles addictions, I can be selfish, self-centered, egotistical, obstinate, and defiant. Usually I would have made a point to let those in the room know that my ideas would work and what they were going to do would be a waste of time and money. Who knows, maybe their plans will produce something amazing and out of this world. The point is that it doesn't really matter. I stayed for a few hours and left when all the basics were decided.

Sometimes life isn't fair; other times it's just a real pain-in-the-butt. Our greatest plans may never come to fruition, and some days are like it was for me today….doing all the right things, having all the knowledge to help out, and being ignored. The bottom line is that I was able to maintain my serenity. I hold no grudges or ill feelings toward those who were at the meeting. I hope the event really is a huge success to further humble me.

When I walk in line with what God has for me, that doesn't necessarily mean that everything will happen the way I want it to. What does happen is that He provides ways for me to grow closer to Him which, in turn, allows me to live a life that is full of love, joy, peace, patience, kindness, goodness, faithfulness, humility and self-control.

Anger is Fear   January 8th, 2009

Anger is fear. When I first heard that phrase, I dismissed it as a bunch of crap. But after chewing on the concept, I totally agree with it. When I looked up the term, I found an explanation of what anger is: "to rattle someone's cage". Fear means to "feel anxious about". When someone rattles my cage, I usually start to feel anxious.

The opposite of anger is peace. I may be getting all analytical about this entry, and the usage of definitions may be confusing yet there is a method to the madness…I think. The point I'm trying to get at is that I try to base my life on the Fruit of the Spirit, and one of those Fruits is peace.

Peace is the one Fruit that I wanted most. Until I got clean and sober, peace eluded me. It makes sense that I was lacking peace because not only was I an angry person, I was full of fear—fear of not being good enough, disappointing my family, letting my friends down, flaking out, etc. The stupid part of the whole thing is that all my fears fed my addictions and in turn, my addictions made the fear reality.

God promises that if I follow His path and remain faithful to Him, all my fears will be replaced. He'll grant me a peace which drugs, drinking, women, and money could never produce.

I have to remind myself that if my life is full of anger, fear, hate, loathing, and all the crap that Satan is master of, I'd better get back on the path that God has laid for me because His promises are love, joy, peace, patience, kindness, goodness, faithfulness, humility, and self-control.

Being of Service   January 9th, 2009

Recently some of the entries I've written have made my parents cringe and want to cry. I wouldn't be surprised if Dad shed more than a few tears. (He's the sensitive one in our family...haha!) On a serious note, it's a testament to how powerful and loving God is that I've been able to overcome and succeed despite all my years of running from Him.

Over the last two days, I've been interning at the treatment facility where I used to work. I've been able to be part of the clinical side and have been reminded on a daily basis just how blessed I am. My stupidity in addictions were strictly my fault; for others, the disease is a by-product of abuse, neglect, abandonment, or physical and mental issues.

Tonight I facilitated a Bible study and was amazed at the level of interest that was generated among the men that were there. The questions, answers, comments, and insight probably helped me more than what I had to offer.

It never ceases to amaze me that every time I think I'm the one helping out, God puts me in my place and shows me something above and beyond my wildest dreams. It was another eye-opening experience that it doesn't matter if someone has been sober for 24 hours, 24 days, 24 months, or 24 years…God is able to use anyone that's willing to listen to His call.

Words in Action   January 12th, 2009

"Confess with humility, pray with tenacity, seek God with intensity, and repent with sincerity." I don't know about you, but I think this is some pretty powerful stuff. Before anyone says, "Wow, Jon, you got some pretty deep stuff to write about tonight," this was something one of the guys I sponsor sent me.

Recently I've been doing one-on-one Bible studies with the guys I sponsor and have seen some amazing growth and insight from all of them. It's kind of like watching a newborn take his first steps and say his first words. Okay, maybe not the same but since I'm still without a kid, this was the best analogy I could think of.

The one constant that I tell them is that there is nothing I can do to keep them sober. It's only through their personal relationship with Christ that miracles will happen. The fact that it seems to be getting through brings me joy. Just last week, the same guy who sent me that text message was the one who was extending his hand to a newcomer.

Here's a copy of the text message session when I complimented him…

Me: "I'm proud of the effort you have put in with Dan. He really liked the meeting and was grateful for what you did. Great job!"
Andrew: "Good just trying to reach out and shake someone's hand. Somebody did it for me so I need to give back."

Me: "Wow, you make me want to cry. Yes, I can be sentimental. Ha-ha."
Andrew: "Thanks for putting your hand out for me."

After this past week, it is breathtaking to see that others are listening to what I'm sharing. My prayer for the week is that those I come across will be able to see me living what the song below says and will be able to make it a part of their own lives:

"Make me a servant, humble and meek. Lord, may I lift up those who are weak. Now may the prayer of my heart always be… Make me a servant."

Realizing What I Need to Work On   January 13th, 2009

I've been preparing a Bible study on the Fruit of the Spirit and have been shown a glaring weakness that I have…patience. I know that the Lord will bless me for all the things I've been doing in California yet I want it now! Being here for six months and going out of my way to help others caused me to believe that I've earned the right to many things. Hahaha.

Tonight one of the people I've known since I moved up here commented that I've been looking sad recently. That would be an understatement. I've let my surroundings dictate my emotions…not good. At the core of my frustrations is my lack of patience. Luckily for me, after the church service tonight, my attitude about things has changed.

I sometimes forget that that people I'm ministering to are still very new to living life without drugs and alcohol. The outlook that I have on life is totally different from where they are. The phone call about when I'm supposed to speak on the radio show hasn't happened and I'm starting to get nervous. In reality, it's simply amazing that I would even be considered to share my story.

In closing, I was just given a swift kick-in-the-butt by God telling me that if I'm going to base my ministry on the Fruit of Spirit, I'd better get my act together and live what I'm teaching. For the last 20 months love, joy, peace, kindness, goodness, and self-control have been relatively easy for me to comprehend. At the same time I guess patience, faithfulness, and humility are something I still need to work on.

Loving Others   January 14th, 2009

"A new command I give you: Love one another. As I have loved you, so you must love one another. By this all men will know that you are my disciples, if you love one another." John 13:34-35

There are times when I struggle to love others. Yes, I can be a bundle of joy that seems to love everyone, but that is far from the truth. Sometimes the thought of walking up to someone and kicking them in the head enters my mind.

It's easy for me to love others when they fit my mold. What I mean by that is when they don't annoy me, get me angry or offend me. The moron that cuts in line at the supermarket, the idiot who talks so loudly on a cell phone at a restaurant, and my all-time favorite, the know-it-all who knows nothing…these are the ones to whom I struggle to show Christ-like love.

At one point in my life I was a "yes man"—never really went against the flow and only spoke up when I was really upset. That's not the person I am today. I'll speak my mind and have no fear of doing so. The hard part is maintaining my firmness while doing it in love.

The thing that amazes me to this day is the balance that Jesus was able to display in all that He did. He was never a pushover, stood for His principles, went against the spiritual leaders of His time, and was able to do it in a loving way. Of course, that's why He's God and I'm a mortal human who just needs to try my best.

It Takes Effort   January 15th, 2009

I used to put a lot of time and effort into my addiction and alcoholism. Out of a 24-hour period the amount of sobriety time would be relegated to when I was sleeping. As amazing as it sounds, from the moment I woke up until the moment I passed out, being high or drunk was a given.

The undertaking to be in a constant state of stupidity was breathtaking. Coordinating drug drop-offs, scheming to get the money, building up a network of bartenders that would deal with me when I was drunk and timing cab rides was like running a business. My addictions became my work.

As much as I really dislike bringing up my past, I share it because it ties into one of my main sayings to those first getting sober: sobriety is easy; all it takes is not picking up that first drink or drug. The hard part is the work necessary to live life without them. For me, I put tons of effort into my habit and I have to put just as much time into living life on life's terms.

There are three areas I try to address on a daily basis: mind, body, and spirit—reading, writing, studying, etc to strengthen my mind; going to the gym or training in martial arts to work on my body; studying scripture, prayer, and helping others to focus on my spiritual walk. Not picking up a drink is easy, but the work I put into my sobriety is extensive.

God is Love   January 16th, 2009

"God is Love." 1 John 4:16

What's the best part of my life today? Before I get to the answer, I want to share what an awesome Bible study I was blessed to lead tonight. The words of wisdom and insight were remarkable. There were only five of us who spent about an hour studying what the Word has to say about love. While I was the one who put together the worksheet and facilitated the meeting, those who participated offered up some interesting and valid points of view.

With that being said, the answer to my question is…a loving family and a great group of new friends here in California. I've shared a ton of times about my parents, sister, grandparents, and friends back home, but God has put some amazing people in my life over the last six months.

I never really wanted to be defined by addictions. The thought that some of the closest people to me would be in recovery would be like me saying that I would one day become an NFL offensive lineman…insane. Instead, God has surrounded me with some crazy guys with stories that are out of this world. Drug addicts and drunks are the kind of people that are drawn to me, or should I say that I'm drawn to….kind of like a moth to a flame.

The majority of the people I'm surrounded by are all like me….born and raised in the church but have had issues with drugs. They are PKs (pastor's kids), people whose grandfathers where pastors, children of parents who were really involved in the church, etc. While our stories vary to some degree, the commonality is that we all forgot about Christ's unconditional love.

While leading the Bible study, I used 1 Corinthians 13:4-8, and instead of using the word "love", I replaced it with "God".

God is patient, God is kind, He does not envy, He does not boast, He is not proud. He is not self-seeking, He is not easily angered, He keeps no record of wrongs. He does not delight in evil but rejoices with the truth. He always protects, always trusts, always hopes, always perseveres. He never fails.

I'm Sick   January 19th, 2009

I feel like a bus just ran over me. Since the last time I wrote an entry, the flu bug that made its rounds got me—not the normal, run-of-the-mill flu, but one that knocked me out for 36 of the last 48 hours. In layman's terms, I miss Mom.

Following God's will is not easy at times; the sacrifice and hardships in the bigger scheme of things are relatively small. The addict part of me wants to make a mountain of my current situation but, luckily for me, I haven't. However, the bumps in the road are still bumps in the road.

With that being said, I'm going to bed. Nothing profound and no amazing stories...just my sharing how having the flu and having no one to pamper me sucks.

Dear Justin   January 21st, 2009

The odds of staying sober sucks. While I never expect that everyone who tries will stay sober, I have a hope that they will. This past weekend I was helping out at a sober living home and the guy I was sharing a room with relapsed. Over the last couple of months we had grown close so seeing him kicked out of the house hurts.

Alcoholism and addiction are a real pain. I'm tired of seeing people lose the battle. The frustration and pain that I feel right now is something I can't explain. As much as I know the statistics, regardless of how many people I've seen relapse, seeing Justin go out is affecting me. Maybe it's that we're the same age, have the same family background, and share a common interest in so many things.

Even though I'm hurting doesn't change the fact that he screwed up. He put the other people at the sober house in danger. The selfish, self-centered, and egotistical part of the disease has reared its ugly head. I only hope that he makes it back to us alive and in one piece.

I know that he reads my blogs so…. Dude, call me or text me. The pain and heartache that you're going through are rough. I only wish I could wave a magic wand and make them all disappear. I wish I could take my sobriety, put it on a table, and allow you to take it for yourself. The fact of the matter is, I can't. You already know what I'm going to say but I'm going to say it anyway…Jesus loves you. We've shared many talks, laughs, and prayers. Please remember that you have people who care for you. At theeffect tonight, people were asking about you and praying for you. You have a family here in California that loves you very much. Get in touch with one of us and let us know what's going on. –Jon

Finding Joy Amongst Chaos   January 22nd, 2009

Happiness is dictated by circumstances; joy is based on the Lord. I try to apply this train of thought to all areas of my life. If the joy of the Lord is my strength then I can find joy even amidst chaos. This was severely put to the test recently. Despite having a close friend of mine revert back to his alcoholic ways, I was still able to not only have joy in my life but also to find peace.

I really can't explain how this is possible other than the three things I do on a daily basis: read the Bible, pray, and help others. In return, God has blessed me with so much. I was able to see through the junk that has happened and realized that through it all, I stayed sober. The other guys in the sober living house stayed sober. Seeing guys in the house really extending their hand in friendship to Justin and offering him encouragement is awesome to watch.

Don't get me wrong, having Justin go out has caused me to question my own faith and sobriety. The only difference is that I was able to see that as long as I have my personal relationship with Christ in order, I have nothing to worry about. It has re-affirmed my commitment to minister to those struggling with addictions.

The lessons learned from seeing his gradual descent back into alcoholism also reminded me how cunning this disease is. All in all, while it's sad to see someone relapse, it allows me to learn even more about what I'm up against.

For some, finding joy in recent events may seem mean and cynical; it's not. I mourn the fact that he's now living in a motel, isolated from everyone. I've cried because he's someone I care about and love. My heart breaks when I picture him drinking his sorrows away.

I find joy knowing that in His infinite wisdom, God is in control of this whole situation. Do I know why? Nope. Do I understand what's going on? Not a clue. What I do know is that it has happened for a reason, and all I have to do is trust in God and keep praying for my brother who is battling his demons.

Snowball in Hell   January 26th, 2009

The insanity of addictions still baffles me. Less than 12 hours after leaving a $20,000 treatment facility and moving into the

$7,000 transitional living facility, two guys relapsed. To make things even crazier, both of these kids are facing jail time.

As I look back on their stays in rehab, it doesn't shock me that much. I can recall one of them saying that it would be cool to get jailhouse tattoos, and that was the guy I thought had the better chance of the two. As much as I hate to admit it, I had lost hope for the other guy from the day I met him. He was just so full of anger, pride, and misplaced blame.

The question I'm asking myself is, "Was there anything I could've done differently?" Nope. The reality of the situation is that some people just don't want to get clean and sober. For whatever reason, they'd rather spend part of their lives in prison. While I have never served any time in jail, I've come across tons of people who have. What I do know is that neither of these two young men realizes what they're asking for.

I wish I had the chance to call them on their crap. It's sad to see that they feel there's nothing for them to live for. Over the years I've met men who have served or are serving time for murder, drug dealing, assault, and armed robbery. When looking at these two idiots who are now in detox costing their families another couple of thousand dollars before going back to a $20,000 facility, they have as much chance of surviving jail as a snowball in hell.

Relapse   January 27th, 2009

"For though a righteous man falls seven times, he rises again, but the wicked are brought down by calamity." Proverbs 24:16

With the recent rash of people I know relapsing, this is a verse that really stood out. Dealing with those who fall and go back to the ways of the world is not easy. Ever since I had a total transformation and got my life back on track, I can't count the number of people I've seen revert back to their old ways.

I have no idea why they choose to allow Satan to get a grip on their lives. How they forget that there's another answer confounds me. What I do know is that I admire those who can admit that they made a mistake and get back on the wagon.

The program that is based on the 12 Steps puts a big emphasis on how many consecutive days of continued sobriety one has. The more time you have somehow equates to what kind of sobriety you have. While I'm very grateful for almost 21 months of clean time, never do I think that I am any better than someone who strings together 4-6 months at a time and goes back out. If they come back to do the deal and stay sober, I give them a lot of credit.

For anyone who reads this and has fallen off the wagon, get back on. There is no shame or guilt. Those are lies that the devil wants you to believe. The God that I know wants us broken and in need. He loves us unconditionally. As this verse plainly puts it, we may fall seven times, just get up eight.

Dear God   *January 28th, 2009*

Dear God,

I have to ask a few questions that have really been bothering me. With the recent rash of guys I know relapsing, what am I doing here? I'm tired of feeling like a failure, especially with JM going out for the second time in less than two months. He's looking at a slow and painful death. Not having a functioning pancreas while drinking is going to kill him. I know this, his parents know this, and he knows this yet the obsession to drink remains. What is it you want me to do? You obviously put him in my life for a reason yet at this point, I have no idea what that reason is.

Yes, God, I know I'm being a whiny little pain-in-the-butt. It's just that I thought things would be different. I try my best to share my hope with others; however, the ones I care about just don't seem to get it. How am I supposed to be this guru on recovery based on a personal relationship with You if the guys I work with keep failing?

Jon

Dear Jon,

To answer your first question, what you are doing here, you are following what I need you to do. While it may seem like you're failing, you are doing My will. Just tonight I sent Megan to pray for you, and what did she say? That you're helping out more people than you know and that others can see Christ-like love flowing through all that you do. For those who are searching for Truth, you are directing them to Me to the best of your ability.

To answer the "guru" question, you should know better than that. There's nothing that *you* can do to save anyone; the only way to redemption and a joyful life is through Jesus. *Christ* died on the cross for others' sins…not you. You cannot save the world; in fact, you can't even save yourself. I sent My Son to do that, so quit trying to be a savior and just be My servant.

Love,
God

For some of you who are reading my blog for the first time, I'm not nuts; I just have unique ways of getting my thoughts out in the open. What you just read is exactly what I was thinking earlier tonight. I was so full of questions and frustrations.

It really sucks to see someone you care about and have been working with go back and start drinking again. The hardest part through it all was that after I received a phone call from JM's dad that he had relapsed, I went over to his house to talk to him. When he saw me, he ignored me and walked away from me. It was like having a knife stuck in my heart.

Dejected and sad, I went to theeffect (a recovery based ministry) and went up for prayer. After crying like a baby and having a pastor pray over me, a few of the people I've met rallied around me. Some prayed, others offered words of encouragement, and those close to me just gave me a hug.

While everyone was supportive, what Megan and Karen told me answered every question. They said that they see Christ-like love coming from me and that I've touched more lives than I know. Sometimes I want to hear God's voice, but tonight he sent two sweet angels to comfort me and to reassure me that I'm where I need to be, doing just what I need to do.

Win or Lose   January 30th, 2009

A few days ago I had shared about one of the guys who relapsed that wouldn't mind going to prison. Well, reality has set in and boy, does he not want to be incarcerated any longer. While he may have changed his attitude about the situation, he may not have a choice anymore.

He knows what it's going to take to stay sober. This is his ninth treatment in the last 14 months. There really is nothing more that he can learn except that he'd better find who his "higher power" is going to be; otherwise, he is in deep trouble. I had the opportunity to talk with him over the last few days, and I told him to quit playing the game; it's time that he wins the game.

Every time I see him I repeat, "Win the game." In the end, that's all this is…a game. There are winners and losers. There is no overtime that ends in a tie; this is sudden death.

The disease of alcoholism and drug addiction has one of two endings: if you win, you live; if you lose, you die. I hope and pray that this young man quits playing to lose and starts to make the right decisions to win.

Very Lucky   February 5th, 2009

A client who's at the facility where I'm working was sent to the mental ward. He was having "visions" that he was talking to angels and birds. He even went so far as to claim that God had told him that his mother is the Antichrist.

While he's been diagnosed as a manic/bi-polar person and the medication will help him maintain his sanity, his drug abuse played a role in where he is. Who knows how much longer I had before I would've gone a little nuts. That's not to say that I don't have problems; it's just that I don't hear voices or have "visions."

God's been so good to me. His mercy and grace are evident each time I hear of someone relapsing or going to the mental ward. The love that He has poured out on me is so unwarranted yet so greatly appreciated. What separates me from those who just don't seem to get this recovery thing? I have no clue. I'll probably ask God when I go to heaven. But until that day comes, I'm eternally grateful for what I have and will do my best to give hope to those who are hopeless.

Don't Quit   February 6th, 2009

Today was rough. Just thinking where to start is making my head spin. The guy who sees "visions" came back to the rehab. Two guys bolted from the center. One of the guys I sponsor is still not on the wagon. Another guy I sponsor got into a fight with the owner of his sober living home and has decided to stay in a hotel tonight. Overall a crappy day.

As selfish as this next comment sounds, at least I didn't have the thought of going back to drugs and alcohol. Some days that's the best that it gets. Through everything that goes on, my sobriety comes first. I need to stay sober in order to give others hope. As time goes on, overcoming the obstacles that are in front of me gets a little easier.

So how do I do what I do without getting jaded or burned out? Besides reading the Bible, praying, and helping others, I go the gym, I write these blogs, and sometimes I cry. For years I would hold all my emotions inside; now I just let it out and give it to God.

Working with people newly sober is not a walk in the park. However, I know that if it's what I'm called to do, Christ will be there to give me strength to press on. On my own, I would've quit a long, long time ago, but with Jesus, anything is possible.

Reflecting   February 9th, 2009

Today was a hectic day: church in the morning, Big Brother Bowling Party, and a one-year sober celebration for one of the girls I've grown close to since I moved. While it doesn't seem like much, I drove 100+ miles. For a guy from Hawaii, that's like driving around the island twice.

Since I spent so much time on the road, I reflected on the entire time that I've spent here in California. Even though I really want to go home, my place for now is here. I've not had the opportunity to share in churches or anything in the last six months. If I was home, I could probably have more chances, but my place is still here.

I've been sharing with the guys I sponsor and work with how God's will is more important than my own will. If I could write a script, I would be speaking in churches. Nothing more and nothing less. I know that God has blessed me with the ability to speak effectively and to communicate on a level that can make a difference yet I'm experiencing a dry spell.

I have no idea why I'm not speaking. Quite frankly, I don't care. One of the guys I sponsor had a talk with me today about how he appreciates all the sacrifices that I've made. He said that without my giving him hope he would never have achieved six months of sobriety. One of the wonderful females that I've spent time with wrote me a letter saying that she really enjoys spending time with me and is looking forward to getting to know me better.

Even though I'm not doing what I want to do and despite the fact that part of the reason I moved here was because I thought I'd be able to speak in more churches, and regardless of the fact that none of my goals have been accomplished, I'm where God wants me.

I'm doing what God needs me to do and have remained faithful to Him through it all. For a selfish, self-centered, egocentric, recovering drug addict, turning my will over to God is huge step. The fact that Christ has blessed me with a second chance at life is a miracle.

Pray More   February 10th, 2009

There's a guy at rehab who talks to the birds. This young man is going to be facing 36 months in jail or the plain insanity of being around newly sober people. To say my life is never dull would be an understatement.

As the world of those around me seemingly spins out of control, I seem to be stuck in neutral—not really moving forward with anything, but not going backward. My goals have changed, and the new goals I have are totally in God's hands. In essence, until God opens doors, all I can do is be prepared and just keep doing what I'm doing.

All the business classes I took and motivational seminars are helping as much as a scrawny waif can help a body builder prepare for a weightlifting competition. For the first time in a long time, there's nothing more I can do to further my goals. Well, I can pray a little longer. Hmmm, maybe that's why I actually ended up writing tonight, to remind myself that I need to pray a lot more.

Finally   *February 24th, 2009*

It's been a while since I last wrote an entry. There's so much I could write about yet I feel I need to share what God has shown me over the last two weeks. Prayer.

I no longer feel the call to be a drug counselor. Being that was the main reason for my moving up here, coming back home for good has become very appealing. Why stay up in California when the comforts of Hawaii are just a plane ride away? The answer is that I know God has a plan for me, and it's not back home…yet.

Last week, Buzzy (minister at Sanctuary) said that King David is just like you and me. David was not a pastor or someone in ministry; he just prayed a lot and was obedient to God. This really struck a chord with me and I was able to relate. If there's one constant in what I'm doing here, it's praying for others. While contemplating what the pastor was talking about, if all God wants from me at this point in my life is to be praying for people in recovery, I can do that.

Over the last few months that I've been here, I can honestly say that I've seen the power of prayer more times than in my previous 30+ years—seeing people being led to the Lord, re-dedication of lives to Christ, and just the miracle of some people staying alive. Every miracle I've witnessed is a testament to God's amazing power.

Back at Rehab   February 26th, 2009

Being back at the rehab center has reminded me how much I miss working with guys who are newly sober. The day shift is full of action, but my heart is with the night shift. It's during this time of the day that I'm really able to communicate and offer hope to the clients. The best way to put it is that during the day shift I am BUSY: Being Under Satan's Yoke. The night shift is when I can have JOY. Jesus 1st, Others 2nd, Yourself Last.

Tonight I was able to share with one of the clients who is leaving soon some practical ways to living a joyful life in sobriety and I feel led to write it out: K.I.S.S. Keep it Simple, Stupid. I try to keep things as simple as possible and not over-analyze my disease. I understand that it's a daily battle; however, if I give it to God, miracles happen.

I do three things daily. I read the Bible because that is where I get my wisdom; I pray daily because that opens my line of communication with God; and I serve by helping others. If the King of Kings could get on his hands and knees to wash the feet of His disciples then I can be a servant, too.

I choose to focus on the solution rather than the problem. There are times that I bitch and moan about things (yes, I make mistakes) yet in the end I think about how to fix what is wrong. There's a saying that immature people complain about what they don't have; mature people are grateful for what they do have.

Give Your Eyes   February 27th, 2009

Give Me Your Eyes by Brandon Heath

Give me your eyes for just one second
Give me your eyes so I can see
Everything that I keep missing
Give me your love for humanity
Give me your arms for the broken hearted
Ones that are far beyond my reach.
Give me your heart for the ones forgotten
Give me your eyes so I can see.

  I work in a field where I should have no problem remembering where I came from. The pain, heartache, and frustration that I once felt are still fresh in my mind. When I first heard this song it was at a church where all the clients were sitting in front of me. Even though I have an idea of what they're going through, I yearn to see them through God's eyes.

  Being with newly sober guys for 28 days affords me very little time to really understand where they are in their lives. What I try to do is show Christ-like love in all that I do. The verse that speaks the most to me is, "Give me your arms for the broken hearted, ones that are far beyond my reach." The key being "ones that are far beyond MY reach." I emphasize "my" because those are the ones that it is truly a testament to God's power if changes are made.

Some may say that I'm in this field because it's a challenge for me. There is truth in that statement yet not how it may have been for me in the past. Previously I would have taken this challenge head-on just to prove people wrong, to demonstrate that I could do what others say can't be done. Who I am today embraces being in a challenging field because any success I may have is only by the grace of God. It forces me to be on top of my game on a daily basis since people's lives are in the balance.

Are You Ready to Quit?   March 2nd, 2009

One of my closest friends back home was having a hard time and making poor decisions. Below is a copy of the letter I sent to her:

"If the drinking is no longer fun and the pain is still there in the morning, or when the feeling you had with your first drink is no longer attainable even after you had more than a few, it may be time to quit. How do I know this? Because I still continued my decadent lifestyle long after I knew I needed to make a change.

There's a point that is reached when love, joy, peace, patience, kindness, moral excellence, humility, and self-control become only a distant memory. When hope is a term that has no meaning and fear starts to consume every waking moment, reevaluate everything.

I don't know if you're yet at this stage, but I'm here to help you get through it—the hopelessness, suffering, anger, confusion, and wondering what to do next. I wish I could give you what I have deep within my soul. I wish I could wave a magic wand and make everything okay but I can't.

What I can do is let you know that you have value. Better yet, the God that saved my life loves you more than you can imagine. If you're tired of the pain and the feeling of being lonely even though people are always around, if you want a fresh start and an opportunity to change, do it."

Hawaii vs. California   March 3rd, 2009

I'm home for another 15 days. *Yippee* is an understatement. I can't deny that the thought of moving back is not a good thought. Yes, California is my second home and there are many great people that I've come to know; however, Hawaii will always be home. In less than 72 hours, I've been reminded of what I left behind.

I don't know if my motives for wanting to move back are wrong. There's a certain someone that I really enjoy spending time with. She makes me laugh and smile on a level that I've not had in years. Forget about just in sobriety; it has been at least seven years since I got excited to see someone.

There's a question to everything I'm feeling. Is this what God wants or is it what I want? There's a need for recovery everywhere I go. The opportunities to speak are easier here in Hawaii yet there are bigger opportunities in California. I have a larger core group of people in recovery in Cali yet I know more people who are searching for how to get sober in Hawaii. To say that I'm between a rock and a hard place would be putting it lightly.

Lucky   March 4th, 2009

I just got done with a four-hour session of getting my butt handed to me by my JKD Master. Being tossed around like a rag doll, having the great fortune of being the demonstration dummy, and the humility are priceless. Not training for the last couple of months has been one of the things I miss most.

What made tonight even better was that two of the guys I grew closest to in the school also showed up. It was like a mini-reunion that was totally unexpected. After class we all went out for a late dinner and spent time just catching up on things. Corky is going to Afghanistan in a month and Chris will be spending the summer in the Philippines. On the other hand, I'll be returning to Laguna Niguel.

The reality of the situation is that regardless of how rough I may think my life is, I'm living a dream. My gratitude list in comparison to my two friends' is enormous. I won't have people shooting at me, the probability of getting kidnapped is next to zero, my HDTV is available, and the opportunity to call home will never be in doubt.

Recently I've only been focusing on what I don't have in California and have forgotten to be grateful for what I do have. Tonight was a great reminder that I have more than I deserve and that the blessings God has given me are amazing. Please be in prayer for my two close buddies who will be in some life-threatening situations.

Memory Lane   March 8th, 2009

My two friends Sean and Eliza just got married. It was great to see so many familiar faces. I may not remember every single name, but it was a treat to have a reunion. Over 400 people were drunk or high but I was sober. I can't count how many people pulled me aside to ask about sobriety. What a great reminder of how far I've come and what a blessing it is that I've totally turned my life around.

The amount of partying I did with the group that was assembled tonight is insane. I would be a liar if I said that all my memories of partying were negative. Unrepentant fun and debauchery would not even begin to explain how much drugs, alcohol, and hedonistic craziness took place. What's weird is that while some of my most vivid memories of the bride and groom were not during times of soberness, they are memories nonetheless.

What I'm trying to say is that once upon time, I really had a blast as a drunk and an addict. The only thing is that eventually I could no longer control my addictions and alcoholism. Actually, the only thing I was in control of was…nothing. Despite all the fun memories that I have, what I remember most is the loneliness, anger, and despair at the end of every night.

God has put me in a position to help others in recovery. For me to be truly effective in what I do requires me to speak openly and honestly about my past. There are numerous times when I felt like I was on top of the world; however, in the end, I was in hell.

Major Decision   *March 9th, 2009*

I guess I'll be moving back home in August. Barring something totally miraculous and unexpected, I feel that my time in California will be coming to a close. It's been a wonderful learning experience, full of great friendships and an opportunity to grow. However, I really feel that God's calling me back to Hawaii. The chance to start a recovery ministry at my home church is a dream come true.

There's a part of me that's afraid to go home. The comfort and freedom I have in Cali have been super. For the first time, I didn't have to worry about the salon, driving family around, and the responsibilities of being the oldest male in an Asian family. Coming home will entail not only starting a ministry from scratch but also all the family duties.

Do I know how I'll be making a living? Do I have a core group of people in recovery in Hawaii? Is the move back home going to be easy? Not really, but I know that God will provide if I'm following His will. The pros and cons of going back home make my head spin at times. The deciding factor was that the pastor in church today challenged us to be a light to all the people we know who are non-Christians. I know hundreds, if not thousands, in Hawaii.

On another totally different subject, I think I'm falling for someone. Yes, the guy who hasn't dated in over two years is smitten. Who the heck knows, my track record with girls is pretty horrible. This time around, she's not a club girl, she's not married, and doesn't have a boyfriend or kids. It's sad to say that in the past the previous list would be a given for the women I've been with.

The confusing part of everything is that when I'm with her, I get nervous. In fact, the other night, I had anxiety. Being nervous around a female is not normal. Of course, I've never been sober around a girl that I'm interested in so I suppose it's expected. I've done many things in my life, and the one thing I can honestly say that I've never done is kiss a girl while I was sober. Very, very, very sad.

I made a decision when I got sober that the next woman I dated would have to be special because, in all honesty, I'm done with just randomly dating. I have a list of qualities that I'd like to have for the person I would be in a relationship with, and this girl fits the bill. For someone who is usually really confident and secure, the feelings of uneasiness and uncertainty are weird. Ultimately, it's in God's hands so I'm not going to stress over it. I'm just going to go with the flow and leave it in His hands.

Learning New Things   March 10th, 2009

I'm still learning things. Relationships and communication are things I struggle with. It's really, really easy for me to communicate my thoughts when dealing with anything except emotions and feelings. Talking about how I feel, especially with the opposite sex, is a mystery.

I can be a smooth talker who can charm my way into a woman's heart. However, when it comes to dealing with adversity and being uncomfortable, those are things that I've struggled with in the past. Just today I was really disappointed in how a certain someone was making me feel. In the past, I would have to have been drunk to deal with the frustrations that I felt. Flying off the handle and exploding would've been my course of action.

For the first time in over a decade, I dealt with my feelings in a radically different way. I sent a text which was firm yet not done in anger. Do I know how it's all going to turn out? Not a clue. I did the right thing. Now I'll just let the chips fall where they may.

Maybe I was in a suitable mood to deal with adversity. I had spent the day talking to two pastors that I respect. I was given insight on how to raise funds for what I want to do. They gave me hints on how to be effective in coordinating events among churches from different denominations. Most important was the confidence that they had that I could be a positive influence here in Hawaii. One even went so far as to say that prior to my leaving for California my ideas were not that precise, but now he sees that I have a clear vision on what I need to do.

On top of that, the lead pastor of the church where I grew up asked me to speak this Sunday. It will have been almost a year since the last time I was asked to speak in front of a large group.

Please be in prayer that I share what God wants me to talk about and not what I think should be said.

The Next Chapter   March 12th, 2009

    I'll be moving back to Hawaii in four months. Wow! The last few entries have been fluff—talking about a girl who, in all honesty, was just a lot easier to write about than what I'm really feeling. What is shocking is that I don't like to talk about the females in my life, so that must really tell you how nervous I am about coming home to start a recovery ministry.

    In California, I'm just a little screw in a big machine. When I come back and start this new journey in my life, I'll be building the machine from scratch. To be very blunt, I have doubts about whether I can do this. In fact, I know that I can't do this on my own. I feel inadequate, vulnerable, and scared.

    "That is why, for Christ's sake, I delight in weaknesses, in insults, in hardships, in persecutions, in difficulties. For when I am weak, then I am strong." 2 Corinthians 12:10

    Reading this scripture changed my attitude about everything. On my own, I'll fail with flying colors. But the great thing is that if I'm trusting in God, my weakness will ultimately bring me strength. The next season of my life will have hardships, persecutions, insults, and difficulties. I accept that as a gift. It forces me to rely on God.

    The God who saved me from drug addiction and alcoholism is the same God who will bless the people I come across. He will allow me to see broken and hurting people through His eyes…with compassion. He will use my heart for those who are unloved and will enable me to show them Christ-like love.

Satan will try his best to tempt me. The lies and deceit that will be coming my way are going to test me beyond anything I've dealt with in sobriety. In the end, the upcoming trials and tribulations will strengthen me. As long as I keep my eyes focused on Christ, Satan is in for a world of hurt. The lives that will be transformed will be a testament to God's mercy, love, and power.

As I embark on this next chapter of my life, I ask that you pray for me. Pray that I never forget where I came from. Pray that in all I do I give ALL the glory to God. Pray that the men and women I come across find Christ as their source of strength.

Leap of Faith   March 13th, 2009

I don't know if Justin read my blog last night, but he sent me a verse that made total sense for me… Acts 26:16: *"But rise and stand on your feet; for I have appeared to you for this purpose, to make you a minister and a witness both of the things which you have seen and of the things which I will yet reveal to you."* Even though I have big dreams, I still wonder exactly what God has in store for me.

There have been so many little things that I've been seeing recently that I'm sure returning to Hawaii is what I'm supposed to do. Earlier today one of the people I used to train with in martial arts called me and we had coffee. Well, he had coffee and I had water; caffeine makes me act like I'm on crack. Anyway, he shared how a bunch of his friends are addicted to ecstasy and was wondering what to do. He also told me that he recently started drinking. (These are 16-year-old kids.)

In this day and age, it seems that if you are sober at 16, it's a minor miracle. Everywhere I turn, all I come across are friends that are drug addicts or alcoholics. The despair I see in the eyes of those struggling hurts. It reminds me of the pain and lack of hope that I once felt.

As I prepare for the next chapter in my life, all I do know is that as long as I keep my eyes focused on Christ, everything will be amazing. Since I decided to move back I've revisited old connections that will be helping me set up my ministry. Despite the massive outpouring of help, there's still so much more that needs to be done. Inevitably, I'll need so much more than is humanly possible. It will be only through God's supernatural power that this will happen.

In the upcoming months, major miracles will need to happen. Unexplainable offers of help will come my way. Ultimately, Sanitize Your Soul Ministries will be an example of unmerited favor from God. Please be in prayer that His will be done and that my will be left at the door.

Two Days Remain   March 16th, 2009

I'm going to be honest; there is so much that I want to write about yet can't seem to process all my thoughts at the moment. Hence, this will be one of my shortest entries ever. Less than 36 hours remain in the 808 state and I am at the same time both happy and sad to be leaving—spending time with the family, speaking at the church, reuniting with old friends, and even meeting a few new ones.

There are major changes on the horizon, and this is an exciting time in my life. The next four months will be important as I prepare to return to the islands to start up a recovery ministry. All I can really ask for is prayer that I do what is right and follow the path that God has set before me.

Coming Back to Cali   March 17th, 2009

This is my last night in Hawaii, and part of me wants to come back soon. Another part of me wants to stay in California as long as I possibly can. In the end, it really doesn't matter what I want. All that matters is that I listen to what God has in store. There is a little fear in returning to Hawaii to start my ministry.

"For I will give you the words and wisdom that none of your adversaries will be able to resist or contradict." Luke 21:15

The ideas for my recovery ministry are really outside the box. There's a part of me that's very nervous about coming back to Hawaii in a few months. I've been really working and praying about what I need to do. As I look over my notes, what the Lord has put on my heart is way beyond what I can do on my own.

What is shocking is that I've come to accept that my adversaries won't be non-Christians. They're going to be pastors and those in leadership positions in the church. Part of me is like, "Why will they listen to me?" or "There's no way a church will go for that." What this verse tells me is that I'm totally relying on Christ. Everything is going to be just perfect.

Family   March 19th, 2009

I've been back in California for 24 hours. So what profound things have I reflected on concerning my stay at home? Family. Mom fattened me up, Dad was just being the amazing dad that he is, and my grandmas are still a little crazy. Yes, seeing friends was awesome, training with my martial arts group was wonderful, and being home was great but my family is still number one.

As someone who is recovering from drugs and alcohol, I've come to realize that the people I hurt most were my family. At the same time, the people that supported me most were the very ones I had hurt the most.

Every time I return home, I'm reminded how much they love me. When things are rough, my world seems to be spinning out of control, or I just need a sympathetic shoulder to cry on, it's Mom and Dad who are the first people I call.

I'm really blessed that I have such a supportive family. Others who are struggling have no family at all. Either they've given up on them or they're not around. For those of you who attend church and know of someone who's having a tough time, treat them like a son or daughter. Unconditional love makes a HUGE difference in the recovery of the broken and hopeless.

Blessed   *March 20th, 2009*

I am so blessed. Not a day goes by that I'm not reminded of how gracious God has been to me. Earlier tonight I got a phone call requesting that I come into work for a few hours. There had been a rash of relapses and leaving against clinical advice at the treatment center. Some of the ex-clients have been trying to get those still in rehab to either buy drugs or leave all together.

While reading over what has happened since I left, it's been absolute madness. Over the last three weeks close to 30% of the clients have used drugs, drank, or left before their time was complete. While those numbers are not really that surprising, the fact they have occurred while they are still in treatment is shocking.

If I ever needed a reminder of how sinister and manipulative Satan is, I got that message loud and clear. Almost every single guy who messed up was on the Christian track. There is no end to what the master of lies and deceit will do to attack those who are looking to Christ as their source of strength,

This leads me to wonder, "What is it that these men are doing wrong? Is it a lack of will power? Are they praying daily? What is the missing link that separates them from what I've done?" For a while I was even questioning my core values of praying daily, reading the Bible daily, and helping others to remain sober.

Through all the insanity, one of the guys who recently relapsed pulled me to the side to talk. When I shared my core beliefs he agreed with me. He said that even though he tried to do all three, one was always missing. Even more telling was when he said he'd never asked God to remove the desire. It reminded me of the one thing I did do...I turned my will over to God. I asked for His healing and blessing.

Overcoming   March 23rd, 2009

I got an email asking why I talk about Satan. Below is the response that I sent.

"I appreciate your reading the blogs, but have you ever struggled with addiction? The sinful nature of man is from Satan. When Eve took the first bite from the forbidden fruit, who seduced her? Satan. Realizing the source of my decadent lifestyle also reminds me of the fact that I need to count on Christ as my source of strength.

You also stated that alcoholics need to stay away from other alcoholics. Well that, for me, is not possible. God has blessed me with a second chance, and I feel led to share hope with others. Everyone is entitled to his own opinions, but until I learned to not be selfish, self seeking, and egocentric, I was not living a Christ-centered life.

If you read my testimony and dig a little deeper, you will see that while the "addiction" may still be around, it does not have a grip on my life any longer. Christ's dying on the cross allowed all my sins to be forgiven. Satan no longer has a hold on me. Yet I write about the master of lies and deceit to share with those newly sober some of the truths that I've learned.

I work in the recovery field and see how devastating drugs and alcohol can be. Before you pass judgment on what I write about, take a moment and ask yourself, "What about addiction do you know? Have you ever been around a newly sober person? Have you stayed up into the early hours praying that a guy you sponsor doesn't kill himself?

An ex-roommate of mine committed suicide and another person I went through treatment with OD'd. Saying that Satan wasn't telling them a bunch of lies would be naive and foolish. Yes, our actions have consequences, but by the grace of God we can have redemption and a renewal of our spirit."

4 a.m. Phone Call   March 24th, 2009

I was going to just copy and paste another response to an email from the same the person who was questioning why I write what I do. However, the Internet is down and I took that as a sign that I was supposed to write something totally different.

Early this morning, around 4 a.m., I received a phone call from a close friend back home. She was crying that her ex-boyfriend was doing cocaine. The pain and frustration could be clearly heard in between each sob and sniffle. The advice I gave may not have been the greatest considering that I was half asleep, but I do re-member something that still makes sense today.

I told her that the frustration, hurt, and disappointment she was feeling is probably the same way God feels when we do wrong things. It's probably even more hurtful to Him because He loves us unconditionally and wants the best for us. When we turn to a life of sin, it's like a slap in His face.

The best part is that, through it all, He still loves us. Regardless of the errors of our ways, despite the mistakes that we make, and even though we are of a sinful nature, He never leaves us, and He loves us more than we will ever know. With Christ's dying on the cross for all of our sins, forgiveness is always there. It's just a matter of whether we want to ask for it and accept it.

The Herd   March 25th, 2009

When I first got sober there was a YouTube hit that was about a calf being attacked by crocodiles and lions. The person leading a 12-Step meeting pointed out that it was when the calf ran back to the herd that he was safe. For me, the crocodiles would be the alcohol and the lions signify drugs.

When I returned home to Hawaii for close to three weeks, I had no herd. The drugs and alcohol were everywhere. Luckily, I have my personal relationship with Christ that made a potentially difficult time actually quite easy. At the same time, until I worked on my spiritual life, the "herd" of the 12-Step Program helped me a lot.

I shared last night that the 12 Steps got me sober but that it's my relationship with Christ that allows me to life a joyful life. The two can and should go hand-in-hand. Being surrounded by people who are struggling with the same disease I battle reminds me that I'm not alone, that they're always a phone call away. At the same time, by the grace of God, I'm never alone if I rely on Christ as my source of strength.

Power of God   March 30th, 2009

"There is a cost that comes with the call and anointing of God. When we finally acknowledge that our lives are not our own and that we have been bought with a price, then everything changes. We begin to feel the urgency of God moving us inexorably to our particular part of the harvest field." (*The Hidden Power of Prayer & Fasting* by Mahesh Chavda)

This is the third time I've read this book. Every time I read it, I gain something new and profound. When I came across this section I started to cry. My "harvest field" is those who are in recovery. The stories in this book amaze me beyond words. Hearing of the miracles that have been happening around the world is a testament to the power of God.

I want to see miraculous things happen with those battling addictions. I know that it's only through supernatural ways that the obsession for drugs and alcohol will be removed. The other day I wrote about the 12-Step Program getting me sober. While it did play a role in my sobriety, it was through prayer and petition that the desire to use and abuse was taken away.

I'm not here to blur lines about meetings, church, sponsorship, step work, etc. The purpose of this book is to share what worked for me. If I had to pinpoint what has made my life so wonderful since I got clean, it's my personal relationship with God. I pull no punches when I say that it's the most important part of my new life.

From the first day that I got on my knees and asked for God's mercy and grace, it was granted. That's why I'm putting so much time and effort into starting Sanitize Your Soul Ministries. The "program" has been beneficial to where I am today, but without Christ as my source of strength, I can't imagine where I'd be. Without Christ, I'm an absolute idiot when dealing with my disease.

Another Day   March 31st, 2009

Yesterday was a pretty crappy day—found out a friend of mine from back home passed away, spent a few hours of the day dealing with a flat tire, one of my closest friends was struggling with her addiction—overall not one of the better days here in California.

Even though the circumstances of the day were horrible, I still managed to find and focus on the positives. Frank and I still had our daily prayer session and I was able to visit the gym twice. Despite battling the "chattering monkeys", my friend was able to go back to a state of mind where she wasn't worried about using drugs. The Sanctuary service last night was awesome. And I was able to have a great talk with one of the guys at the transition house.

Some days are better than others yet despite all the junk that happened, it was still a thousand times more fulfilling than my best days using and abusing drugs. Suffice it to say that there is a peace that cannot be taken away as long as I keep my focus on things above.

Trust & Obey   April 1st, 2009

There are days when I completely lose focus. To say that I'm all over the place would not be far from the truth. Over the last 72 hours I've met with more people than I can count. Issues back home have made my head hurt. Feelings of biting off more than I can chew, insecurities about my personal life, and an overwhelming sense of having too much on my plate would be an accurate description of how I've been feeling.

The power and mercy of God came flooding through at theeffect tonight. Two very distinct and telling things happened at this meeting. First, a dear friend basically told me that I needed to go back to the person I was before my trip to Hawaii—someone who was firm, with a purpose, and would not let outside distractions affect my life. So simple yet very true.

What was even more special was what happened during the praise and worship. My brain wanted me to stew over some personal crap that I'm dealing with; my heart told me to pray for a specific person in the meeting. As much as I tried to ignore God and do my own thing, I kept praying for this young man. After each song I would think, "Okay, I'm done. Back to worrying about something I have no control over." Each time, God let me know in His own way, "Nope, you're not done praying."

At the end of the worship service, God put something else on my heart: "Go tell that young man that he is still loved by Me." I didn't really know this guy. I tried to come up with every excuse not to do it. I lost; God won.

During the break I pulled him aside and, after explaining that doing this was out of my comfort zone, I said, "I barely know you, but God wanted me to let you know He still loves you." With a look of shock, he said, "I've been praying for the last week that God would show me that He still loved me."

Sometimes the most difficult and uncomfortable things that God asks us to do shows how awesome and amazing He is. All the initial fears and doubts that I had before walking into the meeting subsided. Instead of dwelling on the crap that I was dealing with, God used me to answer someone else's prayer. The moral of the story is that when I put my total faith in God, He makes all things right. I'm reminded of the old hymn: "Trust and obey, for there's no other way to be happy in Jesus but to trust and obey."

Confirmation   April 2nd, 2009

Confirmation. As I embark on the next part of my life, something I've been searching for is confirmation. I'm leaving a great group of friends here in California. Great does not even begin to explain what I have here. When I'm down, there are people who make me laugh. The rare times that I get "in my head" and let ideas spin around like a carousel, someone is there to point it out.

I had lunch/coffee with a girl who has started something similar to what I want to start in Hawaii. In the course of our talk, I mentioned that I'd be missing everything that the recovery community has to offer here in the OC. Without skipping a beat, she said that she feels the same way because at some point she'll be leaving.

What was really helpful was that she said if God's calling me away from this comfort zone, He'll provide something for me when I return home.

I've been back in Cali for a little over two weeks. During that time, word has spread through the community that I'll be starting a ministry. Each and every person that has talked to me about it says they think that as long as I keep my eyes on Christ, it will be a success.

Random people that I've hardly ever talked to have come up to me. Guys who went through treatment, workers at rehab, people at church… The words of encouragement have been absolutely incredible.

Problem vs. Solution   April 3rd, 2009

I was texting to one of my friends back home and she commented, "Ever since you got sober, nothing ever seems to get you down for too long. After every setback, you always bounce back. Not once have I ever heard you complain." Part of me wanted to laugh. I texted her back that I took it as a compliment. The other part of me wanted to text, "You should ask my parents or the new little headache if that was true?"

What she stated is not that far off. Yes, I still have moments when I want to kick someone in the head or scream, "Shut up, you idiot!" However, most of the time I try to practice this concept: Identify the problem, find a solution, and focus on that—the solution, not the problem.

Is it easy to find the solution? Heck, no. It's much easier to dwell on the problem and let it consume every waking moment. If I continue letting problems overtake my life, nothing good will happen. One of the things I've learned is how to cope with situations that seem to have no answer—I pray and give it to God.

There's a sign posted in many rehab/sober living homes. I paraphrase it like this: "This is God. I will be handling all your problems today. I really don't need your help. Since I will be taking care of everything, have a great day and don't worry about it."

I wish I could say that I do this all the time. In reality, I don't. I still try to take control of things, plan how they should come out, and ultimately, go back to square one. After a few times of beating my head against the proverbial wall, I eventually give it to God. While the end result may not be what I had wanted, it's always the result that I needed. The solution in my life is always prayer. The funny thing is that sometimes I still forget.

Another Perspective   April 6th, 2009

Today was an extremely difficult day. Honestly, I'm in no mood to write; however, I do have an email from the person who helped me out the other night at theeffect. Here is what she replied when she read my entry:

"Wow, Jon! That is really exciting. I am so glad that I played a part in your journey. Also, God is truly amazing and you are absolutely right that He shows us how amazing He is when we follow His voice. Like when I had an overwhelming desire to say 'hi' to Shannon and tell her I'm proud of her the very first time we had even seen each other. I didn't know her, and it was awkward in my head, but not when I opened my mouth and the words came out.

Also, Jon, thank you for showing me God's love. I struggled with that for a very long time. His love shines through you when you speak to others. You are very convincing. Now it's becoming clearer to me when God speaks to me. I never understood that before, but now that I'm seeing it for myself, it is such a blessing.

Look, Jon, no person can satisfy your deepest needs. That's God's job. We cannot find acceptance, approval, or anything like that in people. We just will not succeed. Plus she is not out to hurt you. She loves you, period. It's your disease that you are struggling with, not her, so try not to take it out on her."

Have Mercy on Me   April 7th, 2009

"Have mercy on me, O God, according to your unfailing love; according to your great compassion blot out my transgressions. Wash away all my iniquity and cleanse me from my sin." Psalm 51:1-2

I'm a sinner. Yes, as outrageous as that sounds, I'll always fall short of the glory of God. There are areas of my life today that are still in need of forgiveness. Even though I try to be Christ-like, I'll never be like Christ.

For many years I felt that there was no way I could be forgiven for all the horrible things I'd done. The guilt and condemnation drove me deeper into despair, depression, and disillusionment. What is so awesome is that God's compassion and grace wiped away all my sin. I only needed to ask.

The best part about turning my life around is that instead of beating myself up for all the mistakes I still make, I've learned to ask God for mercy. Plead for his unconditional love and accept his compassion. There's no way I'll ever be perfect. Sin will always be a part of who I am. Despite all my shortcomings and sinful ways, God is always there to cleanse me from within.

Grief   April 8th, 2009

Four guys that I'm really close to relapsed in a span of 48 hours. It sucks. Three went back to drinking within a span of a few hours. Late Saturday night/early Sunday morning, my head was spinning. I've now come to realize that I was going through the stages of grief. Denial, anger, bargaining, depression, and finally by late Sunday afternoon, acceptance.

In reality, I didn't do any bargaining because there was nothing to make a deal about. However, denial, anger, and depression set in really quickly. The two that affected me the most were anger and depression. They fueled each other to the point that I lashed out at Jaclyn (a friend from back home) who was not even part of the problem. When I say "lashed out" I mean I went above and beyond trying to hurt her.

For some reason my mind told me that all the pain, hurt, frustration, and disappointment would be relieved if I took it out on her. Not the brightest or kindest thing I've done. In the end, I was lucky enough that she forgave me for my stupidity and lack of respect. It took her forgiving me to allow me to accept that four of my guys went out.

The field that I'm in will have numerous people failing to remain sober. I only pray that my coping skills with grief get better. This time I was very blessed to have someone who understood my pain, who knows what will happen the next time I lose my cool. While I know I have areas of my life to work on, it's apparent that my actions still can hurt others.

Please be in prayer for John, John, Glenn, and Justin. Whatever is going on in their heads is something I have no control over. All I can do is be there for them and support them in prayer. At the same time, please be praying that I learn to deal with my emotions and feelings. It's not easy yet I know this is what God has called me to do. And as long as I rely on Him, anything is possible.

Practicing What I Preach   April 9th, 2009

Over the last few days I've been stuck in neutral with the same stupid thoughts running over and over in my head. Karen finally had to put it to me straight, again…I need to go back to the person I was before my trip back home. Yes, I already wrote about this earlier and agreed with everything that she said. However, I'm stubborn and like to do things my way.

After finally heeding what she said, I'm in a much better place today. My activities for the day were prayer group in the morning (well, it's only two of us), movies with some of the guys from Sanctuary Home, head shaving, a run on the beach, an attempt to attend a Bible Study (I think Frank had the wrong time or day), and finally, 24-Hour Fitness which included some Jacuzzi and sauna time. This would typically be what I would've done on my days off from work.

The last couple of days I've been staring at my phone waiting for texts and phone calls that never came. My brain was thinking of reasons why I wasn't getting any response. Guess what? The texts and phone calls still haven't come. One of my guys is holed up in a hotel room drinking himself to death. The girl back home has all of a sudden become too busy for me. I'm still waiting for word on what happened to the guy in detox.

Through it all, I'm at peace with everything. Last week I wrote about focusing on the solution and not the problem. Well, I can be a hard-headed moron at times. I'd been worrying only about the problems and totally forgot about the solutions. Today was a day full of solutions, praying, reading my Bible, and being a servant. It's amazing how when I actually practice what I preach, it works.

Happy Easter — April 12th, 2009

As one of the guys I've grown closest to in California always says, the tomb is still empty. That's it. Nothing interesting or spectacular has happened. Just wanted to wish everyone a Happy Easter. Oh, and the prayer requests that I put out last week have all been answered. John is safe in a detox getting the help he needs. Glenn called to let me know he's back in NYC going to meetings and working on his sobriety. Justin asked me to be his accountability buddy, and the other John has moved into a great sober living home and is doing well. Amen!

A Lifetime of Memories — April 14th, 2009

There's a community here in Southern California that is simply amazing. I'll miss them dearly. Originally, I was planning on coming home during the latter part of July; now it's looking like June 3rd. I've been debating this for the last few weeks and I've finally found peace with the decision.

The hardest part of coming home is leaving the guys I sponsor, particularly Andrew. Don't get me wrong, I'm going to miss all my guys, but he is someone that will always have a special place in my heart. I never wanted to be a sponsor, but God put this 6'4" white boy in my life.

As I struggled with my decision to come home early, Andrew called. He wanted to thank me for all that I've done. There were memories that he brought up that I had totally forgotten about and some that I remember like it happened yesterday. He also stated that it was time for me to go home.

It never ceases to amaze me when I see how God works. I finally understand the statement, "People come into your life for a reason, a season, or a lifetime." When you figure out which it is, you know exactly what to do.

Even though I'll be 2,500 miles away, all the people in California will be in my life for a lifetime. While every person I came across was there for a reason, many were an integral part of a very important season, and best of all, I will have a lifetime worth of memories to cherish.

Psalm 19:14   April 15th, 2009

"Let the words of my mouth and the meditation of my heart be acceptable in Your sight, O LORD, my rock and my Redeemer." Psalm 19:14

I booked my flight back home. May 30th, 8:45 p.m. is my arrival time at HNL. Since I found out that I'll be starting a recovery ministry, countless prayers, notes, meetings, talks, advice, etc. have taken place. The encouragement that I've been given is remarkable. Through it all, this verse is something that I most want to live by when I come home.

Without Christ as my source of strength, unless I keep my eyes on Him, if I try to do this on my own, I will fail. It may be a success to the outside world, but in my heart, I'll be empty. I strive to live a life that is acceptable to God; it is His confirmation that I seek, His will that I want to follow, and His finding pleasure in the choices that I make that I hope for.

I know that if I place my trust on the Rock (Christ) nothing can tear me down. It's easy to rely only on human things—what I hear, see, smell, touch, and feel. Yet if I only count on those things, I can be easily swayed and washed away. However, if I can maintain and continue to work on my relationship with Jesus, everything will be amazing.

Considering that I'll be speaking to pastors, churches, and people in recovery, it's imperative to have the words that come out of my mouth be what God wants. As I contemplate and think about the direction I want Sanitize Your Soul Ministries to go, I need to have Christ as the focal point. If I can do these things, the words of my mouth and the meditation of my heart will be acceptable in His sight.

Sad Reminder   April 16th, 2009

Losing someone to an overdose is not uncommon in recovery. In fact, it's almost a certainty that eventually someone you've grown close to will relapse and pass away. The program says it's institutions, incarceration, and death; that's the nature of the beast. The disease of drug addiction and alcoholism leads to death.

Just today, two of my friends were dealt the harsh reminder of how cunning, powerful, and deadly drug addiction is. Their high school classmate / ex-boyfriend died of a heroin overdose this morning. As I type this entry, I'm actually emotionless about the whole thing, while Karen and Nicole are struggling with feelings.

Maybe I've seen too many young people lose the battle of addiction. Part of me thinks that if this young man knew Christ he's in heaven right now. Another part is indifferent because it's just part of the field I work in. Yeah, some may see it as cold; I think I was able to cope with recent events because in some way which I will never know, it's God's will.

How can it be God's will to have this young man die at such an early age? Where is God's will in such a tragic event? Honestly, I can't answer that; only God can. What I do know is that God does not impose His will. He allows choices to be made. Sadly, the decision this man made early this morning cost him his life.

As I look at this from an outside point of view, I'm trying to find how this dreadful accident can correlate to the Fruit of the Spirit. I've learned to show love to others even more; you never know when the last time you will see someone will be. I can find joy in knowing that my two friends Karen and Nicole are seeking God to comfort them. There is a peace that surpasses all understanding as I offer prayer and support to them. As I wait on God to reveal Himself as to why this happened, I'm again being taught patience. I sent out a mass text message to those I know to pray, and the kindness and goodness that flowed was amazing. The faithfulness that Karen displayed when she first called asking for prayer was incredible. Humility and self-control is evident in that both of these young women turned to God instead of turning to drugs and alcohol.

Whom Do I Serve? April 17th, 2009

"Am I trying to win the approval of men, or of God? Or I am trying to please men? If I were still trying to please men, I would not be a servant of God." Galatians 1:10

There is that age-old adage, "Whom do you serve?" For many years I was a slave to money, fame, power, women, drugs, alcohol, etc. Serving God was the farthest thing from my mind. For those who have been reading my blog or who were around when I was partying, you know where it got me—nowhere.

Today I don't have money. I've been volunteering for the last six months. If it weren't for my family helping out, I would have been back in Hawaii a very long time ago. Fame and power…that is just so funny it makes me laugh. Women? I haven't had a girlfriend in over two years. Battling the horrors of drugs and alcohol is now my purpose in life.

So whom do I serve now? God. If it weren't for His unconditional love, I'd be miserable. If it weren't for His mercy and grace, I'd be dead. If He hadn't sent Jesus to die on the cross for all my sins, I'd go straight to hell.

Two years ago I would never have told any of my friends about Christ. Uncool, lame, preacher, goodie-two-shoes, and party pooper are what I thought they would've said. In reality, hypocrite probably best describes what I was. Today I rarely speak about my faith; I let my actions speak for themselves. When friends saw a dramatic change in me, that allowed me to share who I serve….Jesus Christ.

Turning Point   April 20th, 2009

As I come upon another sober birthday in just over two weeks, I'm reminded of how blessed I really am. Before I got clean and sober, I felt alone, left out, a recluse; though I knew tons of people, I felt I was forgotten and unwanted. The depression, loneliness, and hopelessness beat me down to the point that during that last six months of my addictions, I rarely left the house.

One of the main turning points in my life was the last New Year's Eve before I decided to make a change. For the previous 12 years, New Year's Eve was one of my favorite, get-crazy nights of the year. Drugs, alcohol, women, parties, nightclubs, fireworks, after parties, etc. New Year's Eve 2007 was spent alone, in my room with a crap load of cocaine.

I remember listening to *Beautiful Things* by Andain over and over and over again. At 6 a.m., I ran out of coke, there was no alcohol left in the house, and I missed going to my favorite night-club because I didn't want to share my drugs. There's a verse from the song that was totally me: "Now what do I do? Can I change my mind? Did I think things through? It was once my life. It was my life at one time."

I'm a very social guy; finding friends was never a problem for me. The problem was that even though people were around and calling, I was out of place, feeling like I was less than them—scared that if they knew the real me, they wouldn't like me.

Drugs and alcohol had become my best friends. They didn't care about my insecurities; they took me to a state of mind where I thought I was in control, they were always a phone call or bar away and most importantly, they never judged me.

It took almost killing myself with crazy amounts of Jack Daniels, cocaine, ecstasy, marijuana, oxycontin, vicodin, valium, morphine, somas, acid, basically anything I could get my hands on to come to the point that by the grace of God, I can honestly live what the following lyrics say....

I Could Sing Of Your Love Forever by Mercy Me

Over the mountains and the sea
Your river runs with love for me
and I will open up my heart
and let the healer set me free.
I'm happy to be in the truth,
and I will daily lift my hands

for I will always sing of when Your love came down.

Free   *April 21ˢᵗ, 2009*

When you smile…it brightens up my day.
When you laugh…it makes me smile.
When we talk…you make me laugh.
When you cry…I cry with you.

Slowly but surely, the defenses that I've put up over the years are coming down. Yesterday I shared about how alone I was during the end of my addictions. Today I can honestly say that what was written above is how I feel about the people I'm surrounded by today.

The fear of not being accepted is disappearing. My insecurities are slowly being removed. Feelings that I'm being judged are no longer a part of who I am. The only way this is possible is that now I know who I am, and I know whose I am. I'm a new creation because of the sacrifice that Jesus made on the cross.

"Therefore, if anyone is in Christ, he is a new creation; the old has gone, the new has come!" 2 Corinthians 5:17

Who I am today is a complete 180-degree change from who I was before. The truth, that is the Word of God, has set me free. I'm free to share my experience, strength, and hope. I'm free to speak confidently in what I know is truth. I'm free to pray with those I meet. I'm free to share that Jesus is my source of strength. I'm free to give hope to others. And most importantly, I'm free to be me.

Seek Peace   April 22nd, 2009

There was nothing really interesting that happened today. Nothing crazy, everyone in the community I'm a part of is sober. I just wanted to share what a pastor told me earlier this evening: seek peace. For the first time in a while, chaos here in California has been absent. Yet for whatever reason, I was still lacking peace.

I mean there are things that are happening back home that are weighing heavily on my mind, but there's nothing I can do about them. Yes, I can still be a genius when dealing with difficulties. What frustrated me even more was that I've written in the past about having peace amongst chaos. I had to ask myself, "What is wrong with you?" The solution is simple; ask for help and pray.

Today's prayer list is just for me. I'm dealing with a grandmother who is in the hospital and they have no idea what's wrong with her. The special someone that I've been growing close to has been distant of late. She called to let me know her phone is broken but my addict mind doesn't buy that excuse. While the previous two requests are important, I know that the real source of my uneasiness is that I'm nervous about coming home.

As I spend time praying over what I'll be starting in Hawaii, the vision that I have keeps growing. It has expanded above and beyond what I originally thought I was going to do. I struggle with what God's putting on my heart because it's going to take a lot of work and assistance from those around me. More than anything, please pray that the right doors are opened, that I'll be surrounded by team players, that finances will be possible, and most importantly, that I never lose sight of Who is in control.

My Stay in California   April 23rd, 2009

My greatest hope is that when I return home I can make a difference in one person's life. That's right, just one. Who knows, that one person may be the one who will reach thousands. As I'm wrapping up my stay in California, I'm reflecting on the people that I've come across. Through it all, if I've been a positive influence on someone, my stay here was worth it.

As I write this entry, I know that of the guys that I've sponsored, Andrew and David have nine months; Ed, six months; Rhyse, five months; Bryan, five months; and my two Johns are really doing the deal. The most common question that I've asked is, "What is so different with me as sponsor?" The same answer has been given each time: I emphasize a personal relationship with Christ.

Do I have a hope that each of these men will stay sober? Of course. I know that *"I can do all things through Christ who strengthens me." Philippians 4:13.* Do I know if each of these men will be sober for the rest of their lives? Unless they have a strong relationship with God, probably not.

Drugs Kill   April 25th, 2009

Drug addictions suck. I accompanied one of the guys who lives at a sober living house to the funeral of one of his closest friends. I'd never met this young man who died of a heroin overdose yet I caught myself crying a few times. The pain, despair, sadness, and hopelessness that filled the room were overwhelming.

I can't count how many drunk or high kids were at the funeral. For them, getting loaded was how they dealt with the death of a friend. As I sat there, all I could do and all I did do, was pray that this tragic event could make a life-changing, life-saving effect on someone who was there.

What got to me the most was the video presentation that was playing on the TV. Here was a good looking, happy young man who seemed to transform with each and every picture. His wonderful smile turned into an evil smirk. The hope and joy that was once present disappeared into being lost. Most telling was his eyes, once so full of life, and in the end, sunken, with a blank and fearful stare.

Drugs kill. For some, it leads to a physical death, but for those battling addictions, it kills our mind and soul first. It broke my heart to see so many young people dealing with the death of a close friend. For all the tears, sobs, crying, and grief, I can only hope that one life was changed by this death. I know one life that was changed: mine. It reinforced what I feel led to do, and that is to bring hope to those fighting a killing disease.

Godfather   April 27th, 2009

I will become a father in four months! Relax, I've been asked to be a godfather for Andrew & Roshelle's son who will be brought into this world on August 24th. The reason I'm so excited is that there was no way I would've been asked to do something like this two years ago. The fact that this couple would trust me to watch over their child if anything ever happens to them still baffles me.

I'm going to miss the community I've been so blessed to be a part of here in Southern California. It saddens me that in 34 short days, I'll be leaving some awesome friends. Over the last nine months, I've met some wonderful people who are committed to living a life free of drugs and alcohol. In reality, I have more sober friends here than I do in Hawaii. The hardest part of leaving is that

I've grown extremely close to the guys I sponsor. Eric, the owner of the sober living home, commented that he'd never seen a sponsor do as much as I do or be so emotionally invested.

When I got back from rehab, I had a solid support network set up back home that watched over me. If it weren't for Dave Giomi, Robert Miller, and Kaala Souza offering me not only advice but also spending time with me, taking me to lunch, Bible study, martial arts, and working out, who knows where I'd be today. The template for what I've done here was started a long time ago by those three pastors. They not only preach the Word of God; they also practice it.

Filling the Void   April 28th, 2009

Did I have fun during my days of partying? Of course. For the first ten years it was a blast. The late nights, crazy club scene, girls, and a lifetime of memories. Well, the memories are debatable. When someone gets as drunk and high as I used to, everything becomes a blur.

For some odd reason I feel the need to share that not all of my partying days were miserable. At the same time, regardless of how much fun I was having, there was always a void in my heart and soul. No matter how much drugs and alcohol I did, that void was never filled. It was like chasing after a sports car while riding a bicycle....pointless.

There are no more late nights that last 'til the sun comes up. There have been more snowfalls in Hawaii than I've had women in my life since I got sober (okay, that's an exaggeration). The club lifestyle doesn't appeal to me anymore, but that void that I was trying to fill is no longer a void.

The days of chasing a feeling that eluded me are now over. What made the difference? How was that void filled? My personal relationship with Jesus. I know who I am in Christ and that is someone that is loved and forgiven. There is no record of wrongs, and most importantly, I have hope that as long as I keep my eyes focused on Truth, my life will continue to be amazing.

Email with Dad   April 29th, 2009

Here is an email thread between my Dad and me. Today was a rough day, which I will write about tomorrow, but until I have an epiphany on how to share what happened, this email will suffice.

Son,

Looking back, life for us during those days are also blurred. Feel like I didn't do enough to help you. I like the young man you are today, have been for almost 1 year, 11 months, 3 weeks.

Love you,
Dad

Dad,

Just remember that if it wasn't for that prayer you prayed in the office 2 yrs ago, I would not be where I am today. Everything happens for a reason. While it would have been nice to never have turned to drugs and alcohol, it has made me who I am today and allows me to bring hope to others born and raised in the church.

For whatever reason, God chose me to be the one to start a recovery ministry back home. I'm so blessed to have parents like you and Mom. Your love for Mom is what I want with my future wife. Your fire and dedication to do what is right encourages me to do things to the best of my ability without compromising my principles. Your undying love for Marissa, Shelby, and me sets an example of what being a father is all about.

Mom's love for God despite her sickness showed me that I still needed to love Him despite my addictions. Mom's dedication to serving her Lord and Savior drives me to do the same. Mom's servant-like attitude, sacrificing her time and energy even though she's sick, makes me go the extra mile for those in need.

Life is full of unexplained events. What I've come to accept is that if I'm walking with God and putting my trust in Him, everything will turn out how He planned it. I see that because of yours and Mom's continuous prayers for me. I'm blessed to have a second chance at life and the opportunity to do the same for others.

Love,

Jon

Effort   April 30th, 2009

Last night was one for the ages. I got a call that one of my guys was drunk at a sober living home. To make a long story short: he was drunk, said he wanted to kill himself, I called the cops, cops came, he got belligerent with them, and he was allowed to stay at the home one more night. After everything was supposedly settled, he disappeared to the liquor store, bought more alcohol, and finally passed out.

The guy last night just couldn't comprehend living life without drugs and alcohol. He said that he's tried and that it just isn't fun. He thought he was a special case because he's so smart, that he's 27 and life has passed him by. In the past I would've coddled him and put things kindly. That hasn't worked. This was his sixth relapse in five months.

After the cops confronted him on the suicide threats and he said he did it for attention, I'd had enough. Basically I told him he was being a whiny, selfish, attention-seeking, pity party, egotistical idiot. Yes, that's harsh to say, but it's the truth. All alcoholics are the same. We're not special; we're just morons when it comes to addictions. Deal with it.

Overall it was a stressful, eye-opening, crappy but fulfilling night. For those of you wondering if sobriety is easy…it isn't and it is. If it was a piece of cake the success rate of people staying sober would be higher. I've worked hard to be where I am. I had to change everything about me, friends, places, activities, etc. While my obsession to drink and do drugs was removed from day one, I've worked HARD at living life on life's terms.

I read the Bible, pray daily, go to the gym, attend church, am active in church, do martial arts, read books, go to prayer groups, go to Bible studies, have gone to 90 meetings in 90 days and still go to meetings, call up fellow alcoholics, spend quality time with my family, have found new friends, have tried new activities, and have stepped out of my comfort zone. I've basically made changes to every aspect of my life.

At the same time, this pales in comparison to the amount of effort I put into my addictions. If you add up all the time and effort on the pervious list, it maybe comes out to 12 hours a day. I was drunk or high 22 hours a day at the end of my run.

Living life without drugs and alcohol is a process of re-learning EVERYTHING—how to enjoy a football game without a beer, having an Italian dinner without wine, celebrating without Jack Daniels, dealing with emotional pain without cocaine, not smoking weed when I can't go to sleep, avoiding pain killers even though my back is killing me, listening to my favorite music without ecstasy.

Sobriety is simple…don't drink or do drugs. Learning to live life without them takes work, but in the end, the rewards are totally worth the time and effort. Love, joy, peace, patience, kindness, goodness, faithfulness, humility, and self-control become a part of life…an amazing life.

Rejoice in Suffering   May 1st, 2009

"Not only so, but we also rejoice in our sufferings, because we know that suffering produces perseverance; perseverance, character; and character, hope." Romans 5:3-4

It's almost laughable that I'm even using this scripture verse today. Rejoice in my suffering? Earlier this afternoon I was ready to kick one of the guys I sponsor in the head. The same guy that was the basis for my previous writing was back drunk and high at the sober living home even though he's banned from being there. I was there when he awoke to tell him that he had to leave. If he didn't, the police would be called and this time he'd be arrested for trespassing.

Here's a guy that I've spent hours upon hours with. I've grown so close to him that I even know his family. Countless meetings, church, lunches, dinners, and drives just to talk about stuff. Before I even told him that he had to leave, he just glared at me, lightning bolts streaming from his eyes. It was like he wanted to start a fight.

As he stomped through the house, all I was thinking was, "I'm going to kick this dude in the head or knock him out." It took repeating, "Let the words of my mouth and the meditation of my heart be acceptable in thy sight, Lord" to stop me from totally going ballistic on him.

The scripture says that suffering produces perseverance, character, and hope. What was really cool about all the crap that happened the last few days is that someone who observed the events texted me: "I think you handled the whole thing really well. I give you a lot of credit for not losing it; I would have." I guess my character got a little stronger.

The most amazing thing is that I also sent a text to JM way before I chose this passage from the Bible. I'd totally forgotten that I'd sent this text until looking up what my friend sent me. After I'd had about an hour to process what had happened I sent this: "Despite what you are doing, I still love and have hope for you."

Prayer Works   May 4th, 2009

How have I overcome my demons? Prayer. Yes, I attend meetings, have a sponsor, see a therapist once a month, and do things to improve my mind, body, and spirit yet if you were to ask me to single out the most important thing, it would be prayer.

My prayer life opens up and solidifies my personal relationship with God. It allows me to tap into my source of strength. When I pray, I know that it may not be answered in the way that I want things to turn out, but I know that all my prayers are answered. Accepting God's answer is sometimes the hard part.

I also want to share that when my church body found out about my addictions, there really wasn't anything they could do except pray. The number of people that came up to me and shared that they prayed for me on a daily basis is amazing. If I were to add up the number of people, it would be in the hundreds. The hedge of protection that they put around me enables me to be in the world and not of the world.

There are days when I'm utterly shocked that I'm still sober. Some of the crap I deal with is crazy. Since I moved to California I've dealt with my grandmother moving into a nursing home, the other grandmother falling and spending time in the hospital, and my mother still battling her illness. I can't count how many people have relapsed that I've grown close to. There have been suicide attempts, guys going to jail, and some even dying.

Despite everything that has gone on, I've been blessed to still have peace. Not a day goes by that when I lay my head down to sleep that I'm not grateful and happy to still be clean. My heart and mind are guarded against Satan. I'm taking this opportunity to thank all of you who have been praying for me.

Two Years   May 6th, 2009

On Wednesday, May 6th, I'll be celebrating two years of sobriety: 730 days, 17,520 hours, 1,051,200 minutes or 63,072,000 seconds depending on what way you want to look at it. Is it a big deal? Honestly…yes, it is. There was a time in my life that I loaded 24 hours a day. I was angry, frustrated, lost, hopeless, emotionally scarred, full of fear, etc. Living life without drugs and alcohol was impossible. For so many years I used to it mask all the things that I was going through.

Has it been a cake walk up until now? No. It's taken a lot of time and effort. Has it been worth it? YES. There's nothing that could change my mind about this sobriety thing. My relationship with my family has been restored. I actually have real friends. The hopes and dreams that were lost are back again.

Who I am today is nothing even close to who I was before. At this time two years ago, my sister had just gotten married and I was having my last drink at Club Tsunamis. I can remember that one of the bartenders that night knew I was leaving for rehab and she wouldn't serve me a drink. I had to scheme to get my Jack Daniels. The night ended with a crap load of cocaine in my system and a girl in my bed while I crashed on the floor.

Twenty-four hours later I was at Pacific Hills walking down the long driveway to a new life. What I know today is that I should not be alive. It is a major miracle that my heart didn't explode with all the drug combinations that I tried. My brain should be a pile of mush (some may say that it is but I beg to differ.) The capacity to carry on an intelligent conversation is gift from God.

I am so grateful for what I have today. God has blessed me with hope, grace, forgiveness, love, joy, peace, patience, self-control and most importantly, sobriety. For those of you who want to know how I have done it: faith, hope, and love given to me by my Lord and Savior Jesus Christ.

Two-Year Party   May 7th, 2009

I had an amazing day. I may be exhausted but it was worth it. I cooked for about 30 people to celebrate my two-year sobriety birthday. It was really cool to have so many people having a great time without drugs and alcohol.

One of the best parts about the whole night was the opportunity to pray with three people. They were not quite sure who God was and were struggling with guilt and condemnation. Two years ago who would ever have imagined that I could share hope?

Since it was a long day, I really just want this entry to be a prayer list for those who attended my party: Brian B, Reza, Joe H,

Joe P, Johnny R, John Mc, John M, Pat E, Tyler F, David J, Nevada H, Brian Bu, Kelly, Ryan S, Stew L, Jay D, Mike R, Matt P, Joel R, Frank B, Brianna L, Megan M, Nicole, Karen S, Emily E, Grace, Lauren, Vanessa, Jenn, Taylor P, and Nick J.

Removing Myself from the Equation   May 12th, 2009

I've not written anything in a while and really have no excuse. Well, I was preparing for a talk that I gave tonight and I wanted to save all my "great" material for what I was going to say. Guess what? Out of all the notes, stories, and amazing ideas I had planned on sharing, none of it was used.

Usually when I speak I have everything memorized. The scripture, anecdotes, transitions etc. This time I actually felt like it wasn't even me speaking. What I shared, how I presented it, all my planning went out the window. As I stood in front of the congregation, I was lost.

Luckily for me, there was a song to be played in the middle of my sermon. I thought I had regained my composure and would be able to get back on track and use my notes; I was wrong. Once again I felt like a babbling idiot. Despite the fact that my brain was telling me I was a moron, my heart felt led to keep on sharing.

When it was all said and done, I slumped in my chair. Embarrassed and ashamed would probably be the best way to describe how I was feeling. This was not one of my finer presentations; in actuality, it was the most deflating talk I'd ever given.

Then something unexpected happened. People came up to me and thanked me for what I had spoken about. Others said that they were crying. A guy that I'd never met said that was the most "real" message he'd heard in a long time. Most telling was when a new friend came up to me and said she felt God was speaking to her.

As I reflect on what I talked about, the one and only thing I remember is that before I went up I was praying with the church leaders that I would remove myself from the equation and let God speak through me. Right before I spoke I started with, *"Let the words of my mouth and the meditations of my heart be acceptable in thy sight, O Lord."* I guess God heard my prayer because nothing I said tonight was what I had planned on sharing.

18 Days Remain   May 13th, 2009

Less than 18 days remain before I return home. While I'm excited and eager to start my ministry in Hawaii, I realize that I'm going to miss what I have here in California. The community that I've been blessed to be a part of will leave a void in my life. I hope to be able to find something similar back on the rock, but I doubt it will be the same.

Last night when I spoke there were SO many people that came out to support me. They even brought their friends to hear what I had to share. As I reflect back on the last 10 months that I've been here, 90% of my memories are great ones.

Monday nights have been spent with the Sanctuary Church crew, Tuesdays at theeffect, Wednesdays kicking it at Frank's house, Thursday is dinner somewhere nice, Fridays have been Aragon & Sanctuary House, Saturdays BBQs, and Sundays my relax day. Through it all I've grown close to friends who I now view as family.

What will happen when I return? I have no idea. All I do know is that if God has allowed me to become part of such an amazing group here in California, He'll provide a group for me back home.

Grace's Email   May 13th, 2009

Here's an email that I had with someone who was at my talk at Sanctuary the other night.

Me: I just wanted to thank you for what you shared with me after I did my talk. It really meant a lot to me.

Grace: Of course! Like I said tonight, I'm not the type of person to give compliments freely. They have to be deserved. God really spoke to me through what you spoke about and it was neat to see your humility and love for the Lord. I have become so jaded about Christianity and people who believe in God, but my ears were really open to everything you shared about and it was awesome. So thank you. Truly.

In No Mood to Write   May 14th, 2009

One of my guys is going back home on Friday. It sucks that over the last three months I've grown really close to him. Despite the fact that I'll be going home in 17 days, the selfish side of me wants him to stay. The bottom line is that it's time that he goes home.

With that being said, I'm really not in the mood to write. Therefore, I'm just going to share a song that I really love:

How Great Thou Art by Carl Boberg

O Lord my God, when I in awesome wonder,
Consider all the worlds Thy Hands have made;

I see the stars, I hear the rolling thunder,
Thy power throughout the universe displayed.

When through the woods and forest glades I wander,
And hear the birds sing sweetly in the trees.
When I look down, from lofty mountain grandeur
And see the brook, and feel the gentle breeze.

And when I think that God His Son not sparing;
Sent Him to die, I scarce can take it in;
That on the Cross, my burden gladly bearing,
He bled and died to take away my sin.

When Christ shall come, with shout of acclamation,
And take me home, what joy shall fill my heart.
Then I shall bow, in humble adoration,
And then proclaim: "My God, how great Thou art!"

Then sings my soul, My Saviour God, to Thee,
How great Thou art, How great Thou art.
Then sings my soul, My Saviour God, to Thee,
How great Thou art, How great Thou art!

What I've Learned   May 15th, 2009

As the countdown to my return is closing in on single digits, my ability to write is diminishing. No clue why but it has given me an opportunity to share some observations about different addictions. This is nothing clinical or by a professional, just my opinion based on what I've seen.

Cocaine Addiction: Well, since this was what ultimately brought me to treatment, I'm really biased. Coke sucks. Looking back on my addiction, it was the fastest and most dramatic fall with any drug I ever did.

Alcoholism: This one confuses yet makes a lot of sense of why people seem to relapse. It's legal, easily accessible, and the stigma attached to it isn't like drug addiction. Out of all the guys that I've worked with, drinking will come before going back to drugs.

Heroin Addiction: I never did this drug (one of the few) so I have no idea what it does. All I do know is that I've seen alcoholics well into their late 70's come through treatment yet I've never seen a heroin junkie past the age of 30.

Marijuana Addiction: When they say this is the gateway drug, they're not far from the truth. My drug use did start with weed and ended with coke. I've also seen an 18-year-old who came to treatment for weed and within one week left treatment and is now hooked on heroin.

Meth Addiction: These guys are crazy. For whatever reason, those I've come across who are on meth are violent, manic, can't think straight, and how they process things just isn't normal.

Opiate (painkillers) & benzodiazepines: Much like alcoholics, those who are hooked on these have a disadvantage since they can get them from a physician. Taken as prescribed, they're not a problem. I've met people who take a whole bottle in a day.

Possible Last Entry for a While   May 18th, 2009

For the last week or so, my writings have been pretty lame: guys relapsing, moving, and I just found out that my ex-roommate from treatment is in jail. All of these have taken a toll. I think I'll be taking a break from writing for a while. If anyone has any questions, comments, or suggestions on what you would like me to write about, let me know.

Over the last 200+ entries, I've pretty much shared everything about my story and what I've learned. I guess it really is time to go home and start the next chapter of my life because there really is nothing left to write about here in California.

My Gratitude List   May 20th, 2009

There's been a drought in my writing as of late. Some of my excuses are, "I'm busy getting ready to come home, planning what I will be doing when I return, a little nervous about the move, I'm spending time with the people I've grown close too." While they all have validity, they're just excuses.

I want to take the time tonight to thank all those who have played a huge role in my life. Without the help, guidance, advice, and relationships that I've formed, I would not be where I am today.

First, I need to thank my first-ever sponsor, Ty. While there have been bumps in the road, this man stood by my side from the start. I also want to thank all the workers who were at Pac Hills when I was a client: Tim, Ed, Stew, Mike, Rick, Nina, Bruce, Anne, and Sally. They were there when I was at my weakest and showed me the tough love that I needed.

My family and friends back home kept me safe and sane when I returned from rehab. Dad, Mom, Marissa, Shelby, and all my grandmothers, aunts, uncles, and cousins. The love and understanding you all gave to me is priceless. To the workers at the salon, I love you all.

I have so many friends that supported me when I came home. You're the best! Marci, Jaclyn, Kelsie, Cori, Briana, Tiffani, Michelle, Mark, Liza, (if I left anyone out, I'm sorry) All the lunches, dinners, hikes, text messages, and phone calls offering words of encouragement will never be forgotten.

To the newest additions in my life here in California, you have made the last 11 months of my life amazing. While I'm excited to be returning home, it saddens me that I'll be leaving such an awesome group of people. Never in my wildest dreams could I have thought that I would ever have a second home...well, I do now. Andrew, Frank, Vaughn, Justin, John, Megan, Jamie, Brianna, Karen, Tanner, Eric, Buzzy, Johnny, Reza, Kevin, Matt, Taylor, David, Bill, Jeff, Tony, David, Tyler, Brian, Ryan, Emily, Grace, Chelsea, Josh, Nick, John, Bryan, Beth, Chris, Pablo, Noel, Joel, (once again if I left anyone out from Sanctuary and theeffect...I'm sorry), you are my family here in California. The hardest thing is that, for once in my life, I have a community of sober people that I trust with my life. Thank you for embracing me and accepting me, a former drunk drug addict that knew no one when I moved here.

Changes   May 21st, 2009

Open the eyes of my heart Lord, I want to see you. With changes coming in just a few days, this is the prayer of my heart. If there is anything that I've learned, it's that I need to keep my eyes focused on Christ. When I lose sight of Him, I get into trouble.

Over the last few weeks, random people have been coming up to thank me. They've shared how I played a role in their recovery and can see that there's something different about how I do things. It still amazes me that God is able to use a former drunk to help others.

Through it all, I remind them that it really isn't anything that I've done. I've just listened and followed the path that God has put in front of me. With all the accolades and compliments, it would be easy to have my ego blow up. One of the sayings that I remember from rehab was that EGO = Easing God Out.

All the glory and praise that has been coming my way is undeserved. When some say, "What are we going to do without you?" I hope they realize that it's God working through me—that all the wisdom I share is from the Bible. The prayers that they say are powerful, they can pray themselves. If they're from the heart, miracles happen. When I go out of my way to help others, that's just being a servant like Christ was.

Serenity   May 22nd, 2009

"Remember when you get back that if things don't go exactly as planned, that it's God's plan too. In this life, we only do what we can and the rest is up to Him. Help as many people as you can, but don't forget your own serenity." This was a text message I got earlier today from one of the guys I sponsor. It's amazing how at one point I was the one giving advice and now he's the one sharing some pretty profound stuff with me.

Part of me wants to save the world. Okay, maybe not the world, but at least the island of Oahu. What I've been reminded of is that all I can do is present the tools necessary to live a joyful life in sobriety and set an example by living what I talk about. It's up to those I come across to utilize those tools and build a closer relation-ship with Christ.

Recently there have been a lot of turmoil and setbacks with the guys I've grown close to—running over street signs, nearly burning down a hotel room, making poor decisions, etc. Through it all, I've had to practice what I preach. I can't focus on the problem; I need to spend my time and energy on the solution.

My solution for all the chaos that's going on around me is to keep on praying, keep reading my Bible, and maintain my servant-like attitude. All I can do is try my best and never forget who I serve...Jesus.

HALT   May 25th, 2009

HALT...never make decisions if you are Hungry, Angry, Lonely, or Tired. It's a simple way that I've found is very effective in making sure that I make correct choices. Nothing is fool-proof, but for me, this really helps.

Hungry: I correlate this to not being healthy and neglecting my body. One of the keys to my sobriety is going to the gym and doing things that promote healthy living.

Angry: When my mind is not processing things properly, I tend to get angry. If I actually think it through and find the positive in the situation, my anger subsides when I stop focusing on the negative.

Lonely: Spiritually, I must be weak because I know that through my personal relationship with Christ, I am never alone. Reading my Bible and praying are ways I can strengthen my spirit on a daily basis.

Tired: For me, it's when a combination of mind, body, and spirit are not firing on all cylinders that I get tired. That's why it's so important for me take a Sabbath to recharge my batteries. This is the hardest aspect of my sobriety because I have a difficult time taking a day off.

Coming Home   May 26th, 2009

Turn Your Eyes Upon Jesus by Helen Lemmel

Turn your eyes upon Jesus,
Look full in His wonderful face,
And the things of earth will grow strangely dim,
In the light of His glory and grace.

This is an old hymn that I love to hear. As I sat in church tonight, I just broke down and started to cry. Part of me was crying because I'm really going to miss the worship and community at Sanctuary. The other side of me was sad, fearful, and overwhelmed at the prospect of returning home to start my ministry.

A little angel named Megan whispered in my ear, and even though I don't quite remember what she said, I felt a peace that I'm going home to do great things. At the end of the service, they had a time for people to come up and pray for me....simply amazing.

The father of one of my guys came up to me after the service and said that he was amazed at how many people came up to pray for me. I'm so going to miss my family here in California. One of the guys even said I'm going back to my second home because Cali is where my heart is.

Right now the prospect of going home causes me to have a little hesitation. Leaving a community of over a hundred people searching for sobriety and truth sucks. The reason I wanted to share this song was the part...

O soul, are you weary and troubled?
No light in the darkness you see?
There's light for a look at the Saviour,
And life more abundant and free.

I know that as long as I keep my focus on Christ, I'm going back to Hawaii and all my needs will be met.

Kind Words   May 27th, 2009

As my days here come to a close, I'm realizing just how blessed I am. Over the last few days, many people have pulled me aside to express how I've helped with their sobriety. The compliments have also come in the form of letters of recommendation, clinical staff at the rehab, and guys that I went through treatment with.

I have to say that the one that touched me the most today was from Grace. She texted me: "You are an encouraging person. You don't know how much you've helped me. Your presence is calming...very." What made this awesome was because this had nothing to do with me per se and everything to do with my relationship with Christ. When she talks about my having a calming presence, that is a total Jesus thing.

Another great thing that happened tonight was one of the guys that I did the intake with at the rehab accepted Christ into his heart! When he first came through treatment, a relationship with

God was not a priority. While the praise and worship was going on, all I did was pray. I prayed that if there was anyone looking for Truth, was totally broken, and looking for a new way of life, that he or she would find Christ as the source of strength.

Was I the catalyst in this miracle? Nope, but I know that my prayers were answered. Most importantly, it reaffirmed that when I go home my focus needs to be on living a life that is a testament to God's love, sharing how Christ changed my life, and most importantly, being a man of prayer.

Feeling Alone   June 1st, 2009

"I can do all things through Christ who strengthens me." Philippians 4:13

Currently I feel alone. That's odd considering I'm home. I'm in the place I've lived my entire life and yet the feeling of loneliness has consumed me for most of the day. If it weren't for my community of people back in California offering me words of encouragement, today would have been a lot rougher.

Tired, jet lag, and sadness are what I'm feeling. It sucks…big time. While talking to my dad earlier today, he said that I need to enjoy this time of relative peace and quiet. Deep down inside, I know he's right. It's just that I'm used to being active and always having something to do or places to go.

If it weren't for the time and effort of working on my personal relationship with Christ, I'd probably be in a world of trouble. In the past, boredom and feeling alone would be a reason for me to drink and use drugs. By the grace of God, that's no longer the case. Yes, I can't just stay home and dwell on what I don't have; at the same time, I'm going to use this time to re-charge my batteries and do some real soul searching on what I'm going to do.

Something New   June 4th, 2009

Working on my ministry, re-connecting with old contacts, spending quality time with the family…yet it's a girl that I want to write about. The fact of the matter is that I've not dated in over two years. Telling someone how I really feel scares me. We texted, called, and emailed while I was away, and I'm assuming she knows I'm interested.

Sobriety has taught me many things and brought untold blessings into my life. The last "hurdle" I need to face is relationships. I am totally out of my comfort zone when it comes to this particular female. There were a few times the other night that the old me would've told her how I felt. The old me would probably even have tried to kiss her.

At the same time, the "old me" ended up in rehab. She's different from all the women I've dated in the past; hence, I really don't know what to do. All of these emotions that I'm going through are all new. Why am I even writing about this? Because despite everything that I've gone through the last two years or so, there are still areas of my life that are a work in progress.

There are parts of my way of thinking that are still not normal. When she doesn't return a call or text in a time frame that I deem acceptable, I think she's out with someone not named Jon. If there's a lull in the conversation, I may jump to the conclusion that she's not interested. If there are two days without seeing her…oh boy, let's not even go there.

For me this a growing experience in trust, honesty, and discernment. It's not easy for me to even be sharing this. What if she reads this particular entry? Trust me, she knows that I've only spent time with her so the cat would out of the bag. Sharing that I'm uncomfortable and feeling like I'm not good enough is brutal to admit.

The bottom line is that this is my life. For those of you who are new to sobriety, I am human and go through the same feelings, emotions, and fears that you're going through. I don't know much about where this relationship is going. What I do know is that it's okay. It's okay to be feeling what I'm feeling. It's normal to actually have emotions.

So what am I going to do? The same things I've done every day: pray, read the Bible, be a servant, put my trust in the Lord, and accept whatever comes my way. At this point, that's all I can do.

Pity Party   June 5th, 2009

The routine that I was very comfortable with is gone. Sanctuary Church on Monday was replaced with going to the gym alone. Theeffect on Tuesday night was replaced with my martial arts school with only six people training—not what I was expecting. Wednesday night was usually spent with my housemates for dinner or Sanctuary House which was replaced with staying home alone (well I had Kapua but she doesn't talk; she barks.). Thursdays used to be filled with a multitude of opportunities to spend time with people; tonight I'm home alone…again.

Yes, Saturday and Sunday were great because I got to spend time with my friend. However, for the next few weeks her family is here from the mainland and there is very little time to spend with her. It's unfair to expect her to fill in for what I had in Cali, but that's what I'm doing.

I can't begin to express my gratitude to those I've grown close to in California. Earlier this evening I was having a pity party. Ironically, yesterday I sent out a thought for the day and it was,

"Never yield to the seductive pull of self-pity! Move past it and enjoy today." I obviously didn't listen to my own advice because I sent out a text, "I miss Cali; Hawaii sucks. I want to move back."

They responded with, "God has you there for a time. That doesn't mean you can't move back, but I believe He wants to use you there even for a short time" "Aww I love you! God is gonna take care of you. Stay positive." "It will get better because you are there!!" "You are on your way, and we are always here. We miss you" "Aww, we miss you, but Hawaii needs you."

Real friends. That's one of the best things about turning my life around. Those angels from California gave me more of a boost than they will ever know. Do I still miss them? Oh YES, I do. At the same time, I know that if I could have such amazing, supportive people in a place where I knew no one, then I know God's going to provide for me here at home.

Patience   June 8th, 2009

"The Lord is good to those whose hope is in him, to the one who seeks him." Lamentations 3:25.

I'm learning the value of patience. Overall, things are going a lot slower than I envisioned. There are obstacles that I never thought would arise. In essence, I'm having to totally wait upon the Lord.

For the first time in nearly six months, I have free time. Even though I was able to live life how I wanted, every day was filled with meetings, church, time with guys I sponsor, sober living homes, treatment center, etc. Usually 40-60+ hours a week was spent in the recovery field. This last week, maybe 10 hours was spent doing what I love.

Pondering what to do next and how spend this upcoming week, I had an hour-long conversation with my sister. Her advice was to spend time with Dad and take it easy. She observed that this was the calm before the storm. While I want to be active and doing things, when it starts, there will be no free time. For the next week, I'll spend copious amounts of time praying and reading the Bible. Until God reveals which doors I need to walk through, I'll just wait.

The Difference is God   June 8th, 2009

You can make a difference in the world when God makes a significant change in yours. Last night I was re-reading the journal from my stay in treatment. This was one of the things that stuck out the most. Realize that I had pages and pages of rubbish, but this was something that made sense.

Over the last week I've seen the relevance in the opening statement. I've had opportunities to meet with people who knew me back when I was living life like a party animal. The most common comment was, "Wow, you are so different. There is a peace about you that I've never seen before." It's in these moments that the door opens for me to share about Christ.

Who I am today is a direct result of God. His mercy afforded me a second chance at life. His love has allowed me to live a joyful life despite all crap that life brings. His forgiveness of all my sins grants me the ability to let go of my past. Most importantly, through prayer and petition, there's a peace that I now have that never existed before.

I'm finally at a place in my life where I feel I can make a positive contribution to society. The time I spent in California allowed God to refine my beliefs and allowed me to practice what I want to do here in Hawaii.

Rehab Journal Writings   June 9th, 2009

Recently I found a journal from rehab. One of the assignments had been to answer the question, "What brought me to rehab?" Here is what I wrote:

Be Free by Papa Roach

I wanna be free from this ball and chain.
Be free from this life of pain
Be free from this ball and chain.
I wanna be free from you.
Now I'm full of guilt and shame.
I can't point a finger 'cause there's no one to blame
So I say I'll never do it again. But when the sun goes down
You are my only friend. I think that I am starting to see
I have become everything I never wanted to be.
I'm really getting sick of myself
'Cause when I look into the mirror I see somebody else

That was all I wrote. I was so broken and hurting that I was unable to put into my own words how I felt. How I remembered all the words to that song I have no clue. I know that I listened to it more times than I can remember.

At the end of my run, my only friends were Jack Daniels and cocaine. That's it. I beat myself up and lived a life full of shame, guilt, and anger. Looking back on how I was and where I am today is like night and day. The shame, guilt, and anger that once fueled me are now replaced by love, forgiveness, and hope.

How was I able to have such a dramatic turnaround? I was willing to do whatever it took to stay sober. I took notes when I was in church services. Whenever I heard nuggets of truth that I could relate to, I wrote them down and re-read them when I was down. When my sponsor told me to do something, I did it. Never asked why or argued. I listened because at that point I was a moron and had no concept of right from wrong.

Most telling about my recovery is what I wrote for my assignment, "Intervention to Self". Remember, this was written less than 28 days into sobriety. Hence, some of the language is a little raw but it shows where I was.

Dear Dumba$$,

If you are reading this letter to stay sober, you are really a dumba$$. Don't you remember the feeling you have right now? A clear mind, joy in walking in Christ's love, a yearning to grow closer to God. No woman, drink, or drug EVER made you feel as good as striving to grow closer to the Lord.

Do you really want to spend 56 days away from Happy (my dog), Mom, Dad, Marissa, Shelby, Grandma, and friends? Do you really want to be disgusted the next morning and start the chase over again? Do you want to start questioning motives of so-called "friends?" Afraid of getting pulled over, accidents, arrested? The answer is NO! Things may seem stressful and the thought of going back seems like a good idea. But it's not. Just remember, *"They that wait upon the Lord shall renew their strength."* Isaiah 40:31

Jon

Misplaced Fear   June 10th, 2009

Today should have been a great day: met with my pastor and everything went really well; had lunch with an old friend; at my martial arts class found out that I will be teaching the class solo in a few weeks; dinner was filled with seeing a bunch of friends from years ago. However, one little thing has made my mind spin and be full of frustration.

It doesn't really matter what the catalyst of my anger stems from. What does matter is that it's one of those situations that's simply beyond my control, and I don't like that. Funny how my will still can be more important than everything. The depths of my anger were so intense that my face grew red.

I heard somewhere that anger is really misplaced fear. In this circumstance, that is totally the truth. Ephesians 4:26 says, *"In your anger do not sin. Do not let the sun go down while you are still angry."*

Even though I may feel that I have every right to be angry, that doesn't give me the right to lash out and try to hurt other people. Revenge and resentment are the first steps towards relapse. They're also a sign that my spiritual walk is not as strong as it should be.

My reaction to what happened was wrong. I was full of thoughts on how to get back at the person. I even went so far as to leave some unpleasant messages. Can this problem be fixed? Probably. At the same time, this has happened in the past and I still haven't learned from my past mistakes. That in itself makes this latest episode even more irritating.

The best part of this entry is that in the end, I was forced to look up a scripture to make my perspective change. Sometimes the reminders I need of how to live life are harsh and will have consequences. Who knows how all of this will play out in the end?

However, I can go to sleep knowing I tried to correct my wrongs, and the rest is now in God's hands.

A Really Great Day   June 11th, 2009

It still amazes me that God is able to use me to help others. What's even more remarkable is when someone I've had the opportunity to help has taken the tools that I shared and is now using those tools to assist other people.

I just got a call from someone I used to sponsor. This is a young man who never got past 21 days of continuous sobriety; today he has 78. AMAZING!!! What makes it even more awesome is that he's working at a youth camp as an outdoor guide and is sharing his experience, strength, and hope so that maybe it would prevent the kids he's working with from going down the path to destruction.

When he shared that I had been one of the biggest influences in where he is today, I wanted to cry. The last 11 days back home have not been the smoothest. While things are moving in the right direction, they are moving very, very, very slowly. Probably a good thing considering I want to do things the right way, but I was feeling a little down.

When I was a drunk drug addict, I always wanted immediate satisfaction. What sobriety has blessed me with is learning patience. There are times when I still struggle with waiting for things yet deep down I know that being patient is important. I've shared about the Fruit of the Spirit many times, and in the past have stated that patience was one Fruit that really I needed to work on. I guess my prayers are being answered because, for the first time, I'm being patient and am at peace with it.

Change   June 12th, 2009

"Change happens when the pain of holding on becomes greater than the fear of letting go." Earlier today one of my friends sent me that quote. I have no idea who said it, but it made perfect sense to me. Drinking, drugs, relationships, etc. ...anytime that I made a change, that was exactly what it took.

Drinking and doing drugs was all that I had known for 13 years. Some may say "fear of letting go?" As crazy as it sounds, the unknown scared the living daylights out of me. What am I going to do? Who am I going to spend time with? Where will I go if bars and nightclubs are out of the question? The thought that scared me the most was how am I going to live life without drugs and alcohol?

When I finally made the decision to get sober, the pain was so immense and I was broken to the point that I was willing to do whatever it took to change. I never knew who my real friends were. I was so ashamed of who I had become that I stayed as far away from my family as possible. The drugs and alcohol had even taken a toll on my body. What caused me the greatest pain was my emotional state of mind. I was a mess.

Today all the questions that I was afraid of confronting are answered. I spend my time with real friends. My days are filled with healthy activities that strengthen my mind, body, and spirit. I still visit some of my old hangouts; it's just that I leave before the craziness starts. The most amazing part of how I live without partying? Christ's love.

I have come to accept that I have a Savior who loved me so much that He died on the cross for all my sins. All the guilt, shame, and regrets were washed away by Jesus' blood. That doesn't mean my life is a walk in the park. I still have doubts, fears, emotional scars, and worries. However, when I turn to Christ as my source of strength, amazing things happen. Because as Philippians 4:13 states, *"I can do ALL things through Christ who strengthens me!"*

Real Pain   June 13th, 2009

Rejection. It hurts, makes me feel uneasy, unwanted, not good enough…. The emotions that I'm feeling right now are kind of difficult to share. Without going into detail, the girl that I wrote about earlier this week….crash and burn. Not like how Maverick from Top Gun eventually got the girl, but a real "I'm not in to you in that way" explosion.

Denial, anger, bargaining, depression, and acceptance are the stages of grief. As remarkable as it sounds, I went through all of them in about 5 hours and 15 minutes. Typing this entry is the culmination of a rough day. Hopefully, this will be the last time I write about this female but who knows? At least for today, I'm fine.

I think that part of the quick "stages of grief" deal is that I've been praying about this relationship. While it sucks that I'm not getting what I want, I can't pick and choose what parts of my life I turn over to God. If this is really God's will, I'll accept it. Oh, I tried to bargain with God on this one, but the answer was obvious when she informed me that when she called me in Cali early one morning to say she "loved" me, it was as a friend-kind-of love, not a roman-tic-kind-of-love.

There was the initial shock that left me numb for an hour. I even screamed a four-letter word a few times driving home. I already shared that I tried to make a deal with God a few days ago. (It's funny now that I'm looking back on things.) I was so depressed that I didn't want to eat. I decided going to the gym for a hour-long run would be better. Last, but not least, came acceptance.

Is there still some pain? Will this hurt for a few days? Yes, it will. But by the grace of God, He heard my prayers. Over the last few nights, I prayed, "God, if she's not right for me, I accept it. Please fill that void that will be left and comfort me because I know I'll be hurting."

"Restore to me the joy of your salvation and grant me a willing spirit, to sustain me." Psalm 51:12

When I read this verse, it was exactly what I needed. How do I know that God is real from this verse? Despite all the anguish and heart twisting that happened today, not once did the thought of finding a replacement woman, drinking Jack Daniels, or doing a crap load of drugs enter my brain. Considering my track record, that is a MAJOR miracle.

Lesson from Africa   June 15th, 2009

Recently I've been really frustrated about starting my ministry here in Hawaii. Instead of listing all my complaints, I'll just say that I was being a whiny, lazy, self-centered idiot. Tonight I went to a presentation made by two of the guys who attend my church. They were in Africa for five months.

Wow! After listening to their stories for about two hours, I have nothing to complain about. In a country where 99% are Muslim, no running water, they got robbed, electricity by generators, did I mention that EVERYONE there practiced Islam…what I am encountering here is nothing in comparison.

As they shared what they went through, I came to realize that I am so blessed. Why it took attending the presentation to remember how blessed I am is a reflection of the disease of addictions. My disease wants me to think that I'm a special case, that my problems are unique, and that everyone is better off than I am.

Everyone has problems. No one in the entire world is perfect and without faults. I just need to keep my focus on Christ and allow His will to take place. When I can totally turn everything over to Him, great things can and will happen.

My Choice   June 15th, 2009

I live a very pampered life. I never have to worry about having food on the table. A roof over my head is never in question. The car I drive is nice—okay, really nice. People have judged me for what I have but few know what I've done to get it. This isn't to say that I'm not spoiled; however, I've put years into taking care of my family that most people never hear about.

Why am I even writing about this? My sister said one of my downfalls in the eyes of women is that I don't earn what I have. Initially, I was very hurt and it caused me to re-live what I've sacrificed for my family. Is this a pity-party? No, but it's my opening up about something I never have in the past.

Before I became a full-blown addict/alcoholic, I was a care giver to all my grandparents. While my cousins lived without a care in the world, my life was driving to the hospital for chemo, dialysis, doctors' appointment, late-night ER visits, etc. Yes, I never completed college and it was my inability to juggle care giving with school, but that was the lot in life that was dealt to me.

There are no regrets. Well, sometimes there are—like when people comment how I live a cushy life without a job while still living a life above average. Would I change anything about my life? Nope. Those drives to the hospital with the grandparents are filled with memories, advice, and tender moments that define who I am today.

It was not easy to slowly see those I love drift towards death. For years it drove me deep into depression and ultimately, addictions. What sucks is that if I'd learned to properly deal with emotions back then, those memories would be a lot more clear.

Regardless, that is and was my life, and even to this day I'm still taking care of a grandparent. Would I wish this on anyone? Of course not. There are days when my grandma says some brutal and painful things. My saving grace is not the money or being spoiled financially. What makes this worth it is that for this part of my life, this is what God wants.

God's will isn't always easy. Would I rather be married with kids away from all the family crap? Work a 9-to-5 job that's secure and building up my bank account? The ability to come and go as I please without planning life around what's needed around the house? I would be an absolute moron if I didn't want those things; however, for this season in my life, it's not for me.

I choose to view my current situation as an opportunity to lay the foundation for my ministry, a great time in my life to finish writing my book. Most importantly, it's a time to spend with my two grandmothers who treat me like a son. Not a day goes by when I'm not afforded a chance to be a servant; for that, I'm eternally grateful.

My Dad's Reply to Yesterday's Entry   June 16th, 2009

Jon,

Don't be too hard on yourself. I remember when you were on top of the world, working at Ryan's while going to school. Well, two rear-end crashes into your car while you were at stop lights with multiple visits to chiropractors changed all of that, eventually leading to your reliance on prescription drugs, gambling, and other vices.

You were no angel, but you always showed a compassionate heart, an evangelistic heart. And, partly because of your experiences, when I visited you in May 2007 and you prayed on the top of the roof at Pac Hills for the former biker, I sensed that you had a special relationship with God.

One more thing, at our Sunday School class about a month ago, I asked a question, "Why was it that in high school, the 'bad boys' always ended up with the most popular girls?" The answer from the women in the class was that these guys believed in themselves and that self-confidence is what attracted the girls."

Once upon a time, up to the 6th grade, you were that confident "good boy". You witnessed, you spoke up, you were not afraid. Fast forward to May 2007, and you've become that "good young man". You're witnessing again and you show flashes of being confident (in the right way). Success isn't always measured by a degree or money.

How much is a soul worth? Ask Jesus.

Love you,
Dad

Re-focused and Re-energized   June 16th, 2009

"But he said to me, 'My grace is sufficient for you, for my power is made perfect in weakness.' Therefore, I will boast all the more gladly about my weaknesses, so that Christ's power may rest on me." 2 Corinthians 12:9

There have been many times over the last few days that I've doubted my decision to come home. My sister had a prayer book and as I was reading, this scripture came up and I thought, "That's me!" I've been looking at all the obstacles and things that are very difficult to overcome. Instead of viewing it as a negative, I embrace it as an opportunity to give ALL the glory to God.

This has distinct parallels to my battle with addiction. For many years I thought I couldn't quit. The sickness that nearly took my life is now the sickness that allows me to proclaim how awesome God is. Without Christ as my source of strength, cocaine, alcohol and a crazy list of other drugs would still be part of my life. Instead, my life is about serving God.

"To live outside of God's will puts us in danger; to live in His will makes us dangerous" (Erwin McManus) What an amazing quote. When I was living outside of God's will, my life was constantly in danger. Overdose, drunk driving, being involved in some crazy illegal activities, etc. My way of living was insanely stupid.

Redemption now affords me the opportunity to become a dangerous force. Does Satan want me to succeed? Heck, no. My mission field is his playground. Drunks, drug addicts, club kids, bartenders, nightclub promoters, and the like are the ones that I feel led to share hope with.

I have to realize that all the crap that has been plaguing my mind is just an attack because what I'm led to do can and will change lives for the better. It also has taught me that I need to be even more diligent in praying, reading Truth (aka Bible), and reaching out to those in need.

For the first time since I returned, I'm energized and ready to go. Who cares what others think? Who I serve is not man but a gracious Father who has been so merciful to me. No more pity parties. A feeling of defeat is just one of the lies I fell for.

Who I am is a servant of God, and all I need to do is be obedient and follow His will for my life. When I do that, I'll be blessed. The blessings may be what I want or they may not be what I want. But it will be what God wants, and that's all that matters.

The Last Few Days   June 17th, 2009

One of my friends asked, "How have you been able to deal with the recent adversity yet are able to bounce back so quickly with a good attitude?" Tons of prayer, reading the Bible and books from Christian authors, reaching out to others in the program, and listening to what they have to say.

There's still some residual pain from what has gone on. However, I don't allow negative thoughts and feelings to dominate my mind. My sponsor challenged me to get back to what I came home to do. He asked what was different about my time in California and what I'm doing here in Hawaii. The answer was simple. I wasn't doing the things that I have as my foundation for recovery: pray, read the Bible, and be of service.

Despite everything that I've been through and all that I've learned, one day away from my program is enough to make my head spin. Over the last few days and nights I've been even more diligent in reading the Bible and I can't even begin to explain how much time has been spent in prayer.

My prayers have not been about asking for what I want. Instead, I've been thankful for what I have. My disease is being selfish, self-centered, and egotistical. To defeat it, I need to do the exact opposite. I've been praying for my ministry, that God's will be done. And if I'm to step back and be even more patient, that He will give me the strength to persevere. And that girl that broke my heart? I've prayed not that she would change her mind but that God would bless her.

It's not easy to submit to the will of God, but it's what I need to do. For so many years, I did things my way. I didn't care who I hurt in order to get what I wanted and ultimately, that led me to the gates of hell.

My Tattoos   June 20th, 2009

Faith, hope, and love. I have all three tattooed on my left leg. They're a constant reminder of my journey in sobriety. Each is written in Kanji and has a scripture verse under it. The first was hope, next was faith, and the last was love. They all have a symbolic meaning to where I was in life and how it has changed how I look at things.

"Come back to the place of safety, all you prisoners who still have hope! I promise this very day that I will repay two blessings for each of your troubles."
Zechariah 9:12

A little after 4 a.m. one morning, I was watching a pastor on TV, totally loaded—cocaine, Jack Daniels, marijuana, and prescription pills coursing through my veins. I was already tired of living the lifestyle that I was so embedded in. When this verse popped on the screen, I wrote it down.

I was a prisoner to drugs and alcohol. My mind was consumed by the destructive nature of addiction. Every waking moment was spent scheming how I could score more drugs. I can't think of a time that I wasn't high or drunk. Life had become a living hell.

What made this scripture relevant to me was, *"Come back to the place of safety."* I needed to find a new way of living life and was so determined that I had it etched in ink on my leg. Change was needed, but I still lacked faith and love. Needless to say, I didn't get sober. Forty-five minutes after the tattoo was finished, I was drunk. For those of you who don't know anything about tattoos, that's not a good thing. All the ink bled out and what remains is faded.

"For it is by grace you have been saved, through faith—and this not from yourselves, it is the gift of God." Ephesians 2:8

Almost nine months after I got clean, faith was the next to be added to the collection. The only way I've been able to remain sober is through my faith in Christ. There's nothing I can do to save me from myself. It's only through His mercy and grace that I've been able to have a life-saving transformation. The verse clearly states that it is a gift.

After praying that if I wasn't going to remain sober for the rest of my life I didn't want to wake up, it was my faith in God that healed me and allows me to live such an amazing life in recovery. Don't get me wrong, the disease still remains, but I know that as long as I put my faith in Christ, the obsession has been removed.

"And now these three remain: faith, hope and love. But the greatest of these is love." 1 Corinthians 13:13

Last, but not least, was love. It took me nearly two years to understand and accept love. There are a lot of scars and pain that took years to be healed. For so long, I equated love with lust. It took learning a whole new way of life to comprehend love as an action and not a feeling.

"Love is patient, love is kind. It does not envy, it does not boast, it is not proud. It is not rude, it is not self-seeking, it is not easily angered, it keeps

no record of wrongs. Love does not delight in evil but rejoices with the truth. It always protects, always trusts, always hopes, always perseveres." 1 Corinthians 13:4-7

The more I read and reread 1 Corinthians 13, the more I begin to see the real attributes of love. This verse never says that love feels good, makes you feel special, or that it hurts. Each and every description of love is an action. It's a blueprint of how we're to love others but, most importantly, how God loves us.

Third Step Prayer   June 22nd, 2009

Every morning that I was in rehab we had something called 3G's. It entailed sharing what we were grateful for, good at, and our goal for the day. While it was a great way to start each day, what I grew to like the most was something called the Third Step Prayer.

"God, I offer myself to Thee, to build with me and to do with me as Thou wilt. Relieve me of the bondage of self, that I may better do Thy will. Take away my difficulties, that victory over them may bear witness to those I would help of Thy Power, Thy Love, and Thy Way of life. May I do Thy will always."

For me that was a HUGE part of my recovery. Each time I prayed that prayer, I meant every word. My will was what allowed me to become a crazy drug addict. I had turned from God and done everything contrary to what I knew was right.

My bondage included drugs, alcohol, money, women, greed, anger, etc. I was a slave to everything and it nearly killed me. There were nights I just wanted to give up—not kill myself, but just had an attitude that I was stuck and would never overcome my demons. Through the haze of drugs and alcohol, I had run so far from God that I'd forgotten how loving He is.

This weekend I spent some time with two of my friends who had stayed close to me since high school. They shared that they never thought I would be where I am today. In the end, they had given up on me. I don't blame them. What I find amazing is that who I am today fulfills, "Take away my difficulties that victory over them may bear witness to those I would help of Thy Power, Thy Love, and Thy Way of life."

The man I am today tries to live the last part of the prayer to the best of my abilities: "May I do Thy will always." There are days that I want to do things my way. Waiting upon God isn't easy. Questions of whether I heard the Lord correctly enter my head when facing obstacles. It's when all these thoughts flood my mind that I recall this prayer. I've committed myself to turning my will over to God…ALWAYS.

The Lychee Tree   June 23rd, 2009

I spent the afternoon picking lychee from the tree in the back yard. While I was picking one fruit at time (my dad found it to be comical), I thought about the history of this particular tree. For decades it produced so much fruit that we had to give it away. Fifteen years ago when my grandfather passed away, it was no longer pruned or fed fertilizer to keep it producing like we had become accustomed to.

"Every branch in Me that does not bear fruit, He takes away; and every branch that bears fruit, He prunes it so that it may bear more fruit." John 15:2

Eventually, no fruit was available for our family to enjoy. After I returned from treatment two years ago, I started to take care of the tree—pruning it, cutting notches where the tree experts told me to cut, fertilizing it, etc.

This tree is much like my own personal journey back from drug addiction. I neglected my walk with Christ, and in the end was a mess. Not only was my life not bearing any "Fruit" but it was one that was full of evil and discord. While there has been much growth over the last 25 months my life, it's still like the tree in the back-yard—producing fruit, but not even close to the potential that I or the tree possesses.

In order for the tree/my life to get back to where it's at maximum fruit-bearing capacity, pruning the tree, or in my case, cutting out the unnecessary parts of my life, needs to take place. Fertilizing the tree needs to continue much like how I need to replenish my soul by reading the Bible and working on my prayer life.

I've always made the Fruit of the Spirit and integral part of my recovery. Today I've finally been able to actually "see" the meaning behind Galatians 5:22 and how it actually parallels how a tree bears fruit.

Disorder vs. Peace   *June 24th, 2009*

"For God is not a God of disorder but of peace." 1 Corinthians 14:33

Oh boy, does this verse make perfect sense to me. Another translation says that God is not a god of confusion. For so many years I didn't even know who I was. Since I've been home I've been called a nickname that epitomized how lost I really was: JKO, my initials. When I was heavily involved in the nightclub scene, that was what people knew me as.

While re-connecting with old friends, I've heard some stories about my antics that seem like such a distant memory. The amount of drugs, alcohol, and women revolving around JKO make me want to cringe. Absolute chaos which surrounded me still baffles me to this day. To say that my life was out of order would be an accurate description.

One of the best parts of returning home is when people can actually see a difference in who I am. More often than not it's "Wow, you have a peace about you that's amazing." It's a total testament to God of how far I've come. This doesn't mean that I don't have problems or difficulties; what's different is how I handle them.

The biggest tool I've gained is letting go of things and not allowing negativity to control my mind. It's through prayer that I'm able to get past difficulties. If that means praying constantly, every hour, every 30 minutes, I will do it. I realize that on my own, my life will be filled with disorder and confusion but when I turn my life over to God, love, joy, peace, patience, kindness, goodness, faithfulness, humility, and self-control will be evident in my life.

Andrew   *June 25th, 2009*

The young man that I've been sponsoring the longest has relapsed. There's so much to write about his demise, but I don't want to focus on the negative. Where can a positive be found through all of this?

I'd based everything about my ministry on how I worked with him. My perspective was that if the first person I sponsored stayed sober then I can help thousands. Andrew was my star pupil.

To say that I'm angry, hurt, and disappointed only begins to explain how I feel.

What I have to accept is that I will never be the one to keep someone sober. Providing the tools needed to live a joyful life is what I'm called to do. It's a personal relationship with Christ that will keep people on the straight and narrow. It has re-affirmed my belief that it's through prayer, reading the Bible, and being a servant that enables me to remain clean.

I have a choice to live life to the fullest or to go back down the road to death. Sadly, Andrew has chosen to live a lifestyle that will eventually kill him. It breaks my heart because he was doing so well yet he neglected his personal relationship with Christ which is what had allowed him to live life without drugs.

This entry has been in the making for about a month. It's hard to share this particular entry because of recent developments with this young man. I have to put this out for others to read. I just found out today that Andrew has gone heroin addiction to using crystal meth. He is no longer in a sober living home and has decided he can't stay sober.

Please be in prayer for Andrew, his wife, family, and unborn son. I love this guy like he was my little brother. I wish I could take out my soul and give him the hope that God has blessed me with. Andrew, if you're reading this, call me. Don't be ashamed. I still love you just as much as I ever have and so does Jesus.

Heal the Wound   *June 26th, 2009*

As I was driving to the gym today, I was thinking how it would be nice to have a new female friend in my life. Immediately after that thought, I was reminded of a text message I'd sent one of the guys I sponsor a few weeks ago: "I'm not here to fix your emotional scars, only God can do that."

There are areas in my life that are still raw and damaged. Not only in relationships with women, but a myriad of things—trust issues, whenever the guys I sponsor relapse, and letting go of certain things from my past. There's a part of me that wishes they would all be taken away leaving no memory of the pain that I've been through. Then I came across this song....

Heal the Wound by Point of Grace

I used to wish that I could rewrite history
I used to dream that each mistake could be erased
Then I could just pretend
I never knew the me back then
I used to pray that You would take this shame away
Hide all the evidence of who I've been
But it's the memory of
The place You brought me from
That keeps me on my knees
And even though I'm free
I have not lived a life that boasts of anything
I don't take pride in what I bring
But I'll build an altar with
The rubble that You've found me in
And every stone will sing
Of what You can redeem
Don't let me forget
Everything You've done for me
Don't let me forget
The beauty in the suffering

Heal the wound but leave the scar
A reminder of how merciful You are
I am broken, torn apart
Take the pieces of this heart
And heal the wound but leave the scar

I've come accept that I want the scar to remain—not the pain but a reminder of how merciful God has been to me. "But it's the memory of the place You brought me from that keeps me on my knees, And even though I'm free." There's this thing called addiction that will take every opportunity to catch me off guard. Yes, I am free and healed yet my disease is only a phone call to a drug dealer away. I must remain humble to God and remember that who I am today is a direct result of Him.

My emotional scars will always be there. They're a result of my disobedience and total disregard of following God's will. However, the wound can be healed, the pain will go away. It's just that I have to trust that it will happen in God's time. After all that I've been through over the last 15 years, the one thing I do know is that God's plans are way better than anything I can come up with.

A Talk with an Old Friend   June 27th, 2009

The other night I was out having dinner and saw the owner of the establishment, a friend from my partying days, one of the original nightclub promoters from my generation. He and I had shared some crazy nights out on the town. As we sat there just talking about old times, he asked me, "So does this mean you'll never drink again? Not even a glass of wine?"

I was initially shocked by the question. He went on and said, "Drinking wasn't your problem; it was the drugs that did you in."

Before I could even answer, the manager of the place came up and said, "Wow, do you realize that we only order a case of Jack Daniels every other month? Back in the day, we ordered one case a week just for you."

I went on to explain that at my core, I'm an alcoholic. One drink will never be just one. It would lead to shots, a bottle, a phone call to a drug dealer, and the rest would be history. There are choices that I made in my past which will never allow me to be a gentleman drinker. The lure of living the partying lifestyle will always be there. What is miraculous is that through Christ, I'm able to overcome my demons.

"Do not conform any longer to the pattern of this world, but be transformed by the renewing of your mind. Then you will be able to test and approve what God's will is—his good, pleasing and perfect will." Romans 12:2

Are there times that I miss "the lifestyle?" It's a Friday night, I am home alone with my dog, the night will probably consist of reading a book and going to bed early... OF COURSE there are times that lure of the nightlife is tempting!

At the same time, I remember the emptiness that each morning used to bring—the constant chasing of a feeling or high that in the end was never attainable. I felt lonely even though I had people around me. I certainly don't miss that utter feeling of helplessness that consumed me.

I've come to the point in my recovery that I can be honest about my innermost thoughts. It enables me to see past the immediate satisfaction that can be gained by living my previous lifestyle. Today I have a hope that my life can help others, a peace that despite the setbacks I still face, there's a bright light at the end of the tunnel. Learning to love and to be loved is a process that I've come to embrace.

All the lessons I've learned over the last 32 years of my life have made me the man I am today. I will no longer conform to what the world considers a success. My life is a testament to the transformation that can occur when trust is put in God. Whom I serve now is no longer my selfish and self-centered desires. Mine is a life dedicated to serving Jesus.

Worry About Nothing   June 28th, 2009

"Worrying is like a rocking chair. It gives you something to do, but it doesn't get you anywhere." As crazy as it sounds, I find this quote from Van Wilder to be very true. Are there things in my life that I worry about? I wish I could say no, but I'd be lying. I could probably fill a few pages worth of things that I could choose to stress over.

"Then Jesus said, 'Come to me, all of you who are weary and carry heavy burdens, and I will give you rest. Take my yoke upon you. Let me teach you, because I am humble and gentle at heart, and you will find rest for your souls. For my yoke is easy to bear, and the burden I give you is light.'" Matthew 11:28-30

I make a choice every time life has obstacles. I can worry about them and get nowhere or I can cast all my cares upon Christ. Whenever I remember to give things over to God, amazing things happen. Each time that I decide to try and figure things out on my own, the end result is a disaster.

The Bible so clearly lays out the solution to my problems. It's when I humble myself before God and ask for His divine wisdom and power that miracles happen. I find it really funny that it took watching a mindless movie on Comedy Central to be reminded of how it's through Christ that my worries will be taken away.

There is Hope   June 29th, 2009

I've shared stories of my days of drug addiction. Some are hard for my parents to read. Today may be the hardest for them yet I feel that maybe this one may help someone who has no hope.

One of the reasons I was ready to get sober was that I was tired—tired of living a life that was just hopeless. At the end of my run, the amount of drugs that were being consumed was astronomical. I had a delivery system set up where I no longer had to leave the house. It was kind of like Pizza Hut delivery, only it wasn't pizza that was being delivered.

During the last six months, I began to hallucinate. When you average one hour of sleep, six days a week, funny things happen to your brain. The paranoia that engulfed me was ridiculous. I would hear voices coming from my car radio explaining what street I was on. The TV would talk to me and I would even think that the birds were spying on me. The craziness of how bad things got was that at one point I knew for certain the FBI was investigating me. Certain color cars that drove around my house…they were agents. The clicking sound my phone made…it was tapped. The utter insanity of it all drove me to take a perfectly working cell phone and drown it in the sink—remove the battery and shove it down a storm drain when the voices continued and the cars still followed me. Obviously the FBI wasn't after me. I was just plain crazy.

When I went to rehab and heard the stories of what drugs do to brain cells, seeing MRI images of prolonged drug use, my brain should be mush. There is no way possible that I should be able to put coherent sentences together. The fact that I can go up and speak in front of people without sounding like a babbling idiot is a miracle.

If you're reading this and are struggling with addictions and alcoholism, get help. It's never too late. Even if you're starting to experience the symptoms I had at the end, there is hope. God created something amazing called humans. There's nothing science could've created that would allow me to have a functioning brain. However, God is one of wonders and miracles. I am living proof.

Afterword

Since the completion of writing *How God Sanitized My Soul*, I have continued to update sanitizeyoursoul.org with sobriety hints, how my ministry is progressing, and prayer requests. I invite all of you to email me at sanitizeyoursoulministries@gmail.com with questions, comments, or to let me know of the ways this book has impacted you.

A new aspect of my life is doing 28-Day Intensive Discipleship/Sobriety Life Coaching. Despite the challenges and constant traveling, it's something I feel God has led me to do, and is a part of my life and ministry that I deeply treasure. Below is what the first young man I've led has written:

Jon and his family opened their home and lives to me here in Hawaii to give me an opportunity to live a drug and alcohol free life. Jon has been a crucial component to my recovery in every way possible. Without him there to guide me through the difficult times, I would not be where I am today. Jon has taught me to live a Christ-centered life through daily prayer, devotions, and scriptures. Most importantly, he has taught me these things through his own actions. He has led by example and always practices what he preaches. He knows what it's like to go through adversity and difficulties in life, but also knows the pure joy that you will receive from God when you seek Him out during those times. I owe Jon my life, and I thank the Okinaga family deeply for their unrivaled kindness and generosity.

John McAndrews